Surviving Ministry

Surviving Ministry
How to Weather the Storms of Church Leadership

Michael E. Osborne

WIPF & STOCK · Eugene, Oregon

SURVIVING MINISTRY
How to Weather the Storms of Church Leadership

Copyright © 2016 Michael E. Osborne. All rights reserved. Except for brief quotations in critical publications or reviews, no part of this book may be reproduced in any manner without prior written permission from the publisher. Write: Permissions, Wipf and Stock Publishers, 199 W. 8th Ave., Suite 3, Eugene, OR 97401.

Wipf & Stock
An Imprint of Wipf and Stock Publishers
199 W. 8th Ave., Suite 3
Eugene, OR 97401

www.wipfandstock.com

PAPERBACK ISBN: 978-1-4982-8028-0
HARDCOVER ISBN: 978-1-4982-8030-3

Manufactured in the U.S.A.

Unless otherwise indicated, all Scripture quotations are from The ESV® Bible (The Holy Bible, English Standard Version®), copyright © 2001 by Crossway. Used by permission. All rights reserved.

Scripture quotations marked HCSB are taken from the Holman Christian Standard Bible®, Copyright © 1999, 2000, 2002, 2003, 2009 by Holman Bible Publishers. Used by permission. Holman Christian Standard Bible®, HCSB®, and Holman CSB® are federally registered trademarks of Holman Bible Publishers. B & H Publishing Group (2010-10-01). The Holy Bible: HCSB Digital Text Edition (Kindle Locations 9-12). B&H Publishing. Kindle Edition.

To Rebecca, David, Jennifer, and Michael,
who survived having a pastor for a dad,
and to Suzy, the ultimate survivor and love of my life

Contents

Acknowledgments | ix

Introduction: A Perfect Storm | xi

Part 1: Crisis Readiness | 1

1. "It Wasn't Supposed to Be This Way" | 3
2. It *Is* Supposed to Be This Way | 8
3. Know Your Church | 17
4. Know Yourself | 27
5. Build Up the Levees | 36
6. Focus! | 45

Part 2: Crisis Response | 55

7. Teamwork | 57
8. Tell the Truth | 65
9. Consult the Experts | 73
10. Pick Your Battles | 80
11. Pray | 88
12. Listen | 97

Part 3: Crisis Recovery | 105

13 Faith | 107

14 Friends | 115

15 Family | 125

16 Forgiveness | 136

    Epilogue: Joy Comes in the Morning | 147

    Bibliography | 149

Acknowledgments

I AM GRATEFUL FOR faithful pastors who mentored me at key times in my life, especially Al Lutz and Rodney Stortz; for professors of Covenant Theological Seminary who showed a young seminarian what biblical integrity and gospel humility look like, especially Drs. Robert G. Rayburn and George W. Knight III; for brothers and sisters who have reminded me to run to the cross for power in ministry; for four congregations that have given me the privilege of experiencing, along with them, God's amazing grace; and for my wife and family, whose love, endurance, and laughter have enabled me not only to survive but to thrive as a pastor.

This book is the product of what they, and so many others, have taught me about gospel ministry.

I also wish to thank the pastors, staff, officers, and members of University Presbyterian Church (PCA) in Orlando, Florida, for their support of this project. To borrow Paul's words to Philemon, "I have great joy and encouragement from your love, because the hearts of the saints have been refreshed through you. . . ." (Phlm 7, HCSB).

Finally, I thank my editor, Judy Hagey, for her diligence and eye for detail; and the many friends who have encouraged and advised me in the writing of this book. You know who you are.

Introduction
A Perfect Storm

BEFORE JOY STEELE OF Ocean Springs, Mississippi, went to bed that Saturday night she tried one more time to change her husband Phil's mind. "We've been through these scares before, Phil," she told him. "This storm will pass, just like all the other ones. Don't you understand how inconvenient it is to evacuate?"

It was August 27, 2005. The Steeles had heard warnings about a hurricane heading their way for several days. So they'd boarded up their windows and put their valuables in a safe place, just like all the other times. But Joy wasn't worried. Not this Saturday. Their neighbors weren't going anywhere. Why should Phil and Joy pack up their two kids and head north? "It's such a pain," she said.

Sunday morning seemed to confirm Joy's skepticism. Puffy clouds painted cotton bolls on a clear, sunny sky over the sleepy Gulf Coast town. "Still think we ought to evacuate? Really?" Joy asked.

Phil turned on the radio and suddenly everything changed.

Overnight, Hurricane Katrina had gone from a Category 3 to a Category 5 and was bearing down rapidly upon the Louisiana-Mississippi coast. It was "the Big One." Joy shouted, "In the car, kids. Let's go."

Introduction: A Perfect Storm

Early that next day—August 29, 2005—one of the deadliest hurricanes in US history hit the shores of Louisiana, Mississippi, and Alabama. As Hurricane Katrina lumbered through the Gulf, her winds reached 175 miles per hour. "Katrina was a giant," says one meteorologist. According to historian Douglas Brinkley, "Katrina was no mere hurricane or flood. It was destined to be known as 'the Great Deluge' in the annals of American history."[1] Her tropical storm-force winds measured almost 350 miles across. The National Hurricane Center said Katrina was comparable to Hurricane Camille back in 1969, only bigger. The day before it hit landfall New Orleans Mayor Ray Nagin went on TV and warned, "We're facing the storm most of us have feared." He ordered a mandatory evacuation of Orleans Parish and opened the Superdome as a "refuge of last resort." And if Gulf Coast residents weren't already alarmed enough, the National Weather Service issued a bulletin, which read in part:

> Most of the area will be uninhabitable for weeks... perhaps longer. At least one half of well-constructed homes will have roof and wall failure... Airborne debris will be widespread... and may include heavy items such as household appliances and even light vehicles. Persons, pets, and livestock exposed to the winds will face certain death if struck. Power outages will last for weeks... Water shortages will make human suffering incredible by modern standards... Few crops will remain...[2]

The NWS was not exaggerating. Hurricane Katrina killed more than 1,800 people, displaced about a million others, and devastated the Gulf Coast's economy, environment, and social structure. The storm surge reached over twenty-five feet in some areas. It overwhelmed New Orleans's levee system. Eighty percent of the city was submerged under water. It became the most expensive

---

1. Brinkley, *Great Deluge*, Kindle Edition: Author's Note.
2. *Wikipedia*, s. v. "National Weather Service Bulletin for Hurricane Katrina," lines 43–64.

INTRODUCTION: A PERFECT STORM

natural disaster in US history. The total bill came to an estimated $135 billion.³

Hurricane Katrina was a perfect storm, a lethal combination of high winds, high tide, low barometric pressure, and breached levees that changed life forever for thousands of people.

My daughter and her husband moved to Gulfport, Mississippi, a year after Katrina. I visited them in September, 2006. I flew into New Orleans, rented a car, and drove east on I-10 through Metairie, over the Lake Pontchartrain Causeway, past Slidell, and then down through Westonia, Mississippi, to US 90 on the Gulf Coast. Detouring around the washed-out bridge at Bay St. Louis, I continued along US 90 through the little beach towns of Pass Christian and Long Beach.

At times I pulled over to the side of the road and just sat there, astonished. Fishing boats pushed up by the surge still sat by the highway like carelessly tossed toys. Trees that had survived the storm were still bare. Massive piles of junk pockmarked what had once been pristine beach beauty. Pylons marked the graves of houses, restaurants, and marinas. Old stalwart churches had been disemboweled. And this was a *full year* after Katrina.

Reflecting on Katrina's carnage, I think of the work of a pastor.

Don't get me wrong. Pastoring a church has many rewards. The sights, sounds, and pleasures of pastoral ministry can take your breath away, just like life on the Gulf Coast. It's thrilling to have a hand in God's heart-healing, sin-defeating, marriage-mending, habit-altering, kingdom-building work. On the other hand, for pastors it's always hurricane season. Every day, ministers of the gospel face the danger of an unexpected, devastating catastrophe. Churches can be unsafe places. They are filled with broken, imperfect people. The pastor has flaws and makes mistakes. Many pastors walk into a church naïve about the potential hazards

---

3. *Wall Street Journal*, August 28, 2015, lines 8–20.

Introduction: A Perfect Storm

of their vocation. Like fishing boats during a hurricane, they get battered this way and that by difficult people, unresolved conflict, incompatible visions, hidden agendas, mission drift, betrayal, and sin—their own and that of others.

You've seen the articles and blog posts that say at least 1,500 pastors are leaving the ministry every month.[4] Recent research casts doubt on the reliability of that gloomy statistic.[5] "Pastors are not leaving the ministry in droves," says Scott McConnell, vice president of LifeWay Research.[6] Still, many ministers of the gospel say they are on call twenty-four hours a day, expect conflict, find pastoral ministry overwhelming, lack true friends, and have had a significant stress-related crisis at least once in their ministry. The pressures and expectations on ministers of the gospel are greater now than ever, and many are not surviving.

Some of you reading this paragraph feel trapped in a ministry storm and don't know what to do. Your boat is sinking and you don't think you can bail any longer. Your church is not growing. In fact, it's barely afloat. You feel like a complete failure. You used to feel God's pleasure when you stood in the pulpit and taught God's people. Now the eyes of your congregation seem like daggers of criticism aimed at your heart. You can't stop worrying about what the elders really think of you. You berate yourself for everything, including worrying. You're not sleeping well. Even in your dreams, you wrestle condemning Apollyon. You wake up in the morning feeling guilty, incompetent, and disoriented. Your spouse has shut down; you no longer pray for the church or talk about ministry together. You're sure that because of you, your kids will walk away from the church one day. You've never wanted to watch so much television before. You don't even like hearing the word *church*. You wonder how or when things got so derailed. You've been checking websites for openings in another field. You know exactly what David meant when he said, "Oh, that I had wings like a dove! I would

---

4. Sherman, "Pastor Burnout Statistics," lines 66–67.
5. Stetzer, "That Stat That Says Pastors Are All Miserable and Want to Quit (Part 1)," lines 6–15.
6. Green, "Research Finds Few Pastors Give up on Ministry," lines 7–8.

Introduction: A Perfect Storm

fly away and be at rest; yes, I would wander far away; I would lodge in the wilderness; I would hurry to find a shelter from the raging wind and tempest" (Ps 55:6–8).

If anything I just wrote comes close to describing where you are as a pastor, this book is for you. And if you think it'll never happen to you, this book is for you too.

Jesus promised to build his church. He said that the gates of Hades would not overcome it (Matt 16:18). But for the church to prevail as Jesus promised, pastors need to be better prepared to predict and withstand the hurricanes of ministry. *Surviving Ministry: How to Weather the Storms of Church Leadership* will help you stay strong during seasons of difficulty.

In this book we will not focus on the personal or moral struggles often reported by pastors: sexual temptation, financial strain, marital conflict, spiritual lethargy, doubting one's calling, and the like. Those issues are vitally important and certainly complicate your relationship to your church. If you are wise and hurting, you will not ignore the warning lights on the dashboard of your heart. You will get counseling and find appropriate friends, books, blogs, seminars, and other resources to get the help you need.

Instead, these pages are about the congregational conflicts and clashes that tear you up inside and make you wonder why in the world you came to this town, this church, this mess. In Part 1, we'll talk about what you can do to get ready for, if not prevent, the next ministry storm. In Part 2, we'll assume that the hurricane has come ashore at your church: what should you do? And in Part 3, I will give you four essentials of a gospel-based response to ministry crisis that will help you recover, pick up the pieces, and move forward with hope and courage. At the end of each chapter is a list of "survival strategies" that will help you apply what you have read.

I write as a pastor for fellow pastors. I'll share my story and those of other church leaders I've had the privilege of knowing. Though the stories are real, I've changed the names of people, places, and churches along with some of the details. I'll also tell you

Introduction: A Perfect Storm

about mistakes I've made. I've weathered a few "perfect storms" in my thirty years of gospel ministry. One of those storms was especially destructive—to the congregation, to me, and to my family. I hope that by reading this book, you will avoid a similar ministry-killing hurricane. Or, if it's already come your way, I pray you will find things of beauty among the wreckage and recover the joy of your calling.

I did.

But let me start by telling you about my catastrophe.

Part 1

Crisis Readiness

Chapter 1
"It Wasn't Supposed to Be This Way"

I KNEW I WAS in trouble the day Suzy and I moved into our house in Edgefield, Missouri, to begin my work as senior pastor of New Life Church. It was a blazingly hot, humid July day. The house was a fixer-upper, so we were unpacking boxes, painting, hanging wallpaper, cleaning the pool, and a myriad of other things to get the place livable for our family of five. The phone rang. On the line was one of the elders of the church. "We need to talk to you," he said. So I drove over to the church, where two New Life elders were waiting for me.

"We're concerned about your love of money," they said.

Huh? What had I done or said that made people think I was greedy? Not that I am 100 percent free of the love of money, but where had *this* come from? As they explained themselves, it became clear that there'd been a miscommunication about the timing of my first paycheck. But I left that meeting with an uneasy feeling: Was this encounter an early sign of a spirit of suspicion floating around my new church? Indeed, it was, as events were soon to demonstrate.

It had been a hard move for my family and me. We loved our former church in Tennessee. I'd been their pastor for seven golden years. Suzy and I had poured our hearts and souls into that church, raised our kids through their formative years, built a house, and seen God move in significant ways. The gospel of grace had gripped me profoundly, and I saw it take root in the hearts of many others.

But here we were in a new place, with a new calling. The drive up I-55 had been an absolute trip from hell. My wife cried all the way. I felt incredibly guilty for uprooting my dear wife and children. Typical of me, I told them to look on the bright side of life in Missouri. "We'll visit St. Louis," I promised. "We'll go to the zoo. We'll see the Cardinals play. And just think: Edgefield is one of the fastest-growing towns in the state. What a great opportunity for the gospel." It didn't help.

Within a few short weeks, I was asking myself the questions that trouble every pastor I know: Did God *really* call me here? Was I listening to *his* voice, or my own? Why did I leave a church where we were all happy?

I'll never forget my first elders meeting. We moved through the agenda and then it was time for my closing prayer. I told the group that I customarily get on my knees to pray with my fellow elders. They could do the same if they wished. As I was getting on my knees, one of the elders stopped me and asked, "Why do you want us to get on our knees? Is there anything in the church constitution about that?"

Now wait a second. How could a spiritual leader object to praying on his knees? I explained that biblically speaking, getting on one's knees to pray is a sign of humility and earnestness. But I said, "It's up to you. You don't have to get on your knees." I was simply stunned. And worried. Was every suggestion of mine going to be put through the meat grinder of inspection? My worries turned out to be justified. That's exactly what my five years at New Life Church felt like: a meat grinder.

We went from one crisis to another. An aggrieved husband sued the church. I had to fire a member of the staff who tried to sabotage the youth ministry. I fired another staff member for being divisive and stubborn. Both firings made me unpopular with segments of the New Life congregation. Our missions director, an apparently healthy man, collapsed and died from a heart attack. We had to discipline a member of the worship team. You've heard

"It Wasn't Supposed to Be This Way"

of congregations that fight over the color of the carpet in the sanctuary? Our church really did.

In the middle of everything else, my father died of leukemia. My daughter was injured in a serious auto accident. My son had to have a delicate and risky surgical procedure. Two of our kids went off to college for the first time. One got married.

And of course, the normal responsibilities of pastoral ministry didn't magically stop and wait for those tempests to subside. There were still sermons to preach and expansion plans to discuss. There were still the dying who needed bedside prayers, the hospitalized who needed a pastoral touch, couples who needed counseling, visitors who needed follow-up, staff who needed direction, and lost people who needed redemption.

Other upsetting tragedies struck New Life during my five years there. A couple of beloved ladies lost their battles with cancer. I did funerals for two brothers who committed suicide weeks apart, and another funeral for a man—a good friend—who murdered his two sons and then turned the shotgun on himself. Though these events were profoundly disruptive, most pastors can tell similar stories of brokenness and loss.

But then came the Category 5 hurricane that nearly broke me.

I had figured if we were going to attract a younger demographic, we needed to add a contemporary touch to the worship service. In my former church I had led singing with my guitar. So one Sunday I brought out my guitar and led one of the songs. I kept it up week after week. At first, people welcomed the novelty. Most of the elders were behind me. Some younger families began to visit. Many stayed. Musicians began to come out of the woodwork. We added another guitar player, then a bass player, a couple of vocalists, and finally a drummer.

That's when the hurricane came ashore.

It started with little pockets of people gathering in the sanctuary after the worship service. I overheard them critiquing the music. Just the sight of drums in the choir loft made some of the old-timers angry. Several families left the church. Soon whispers

5

turned to organized protest. To respond to the complaints, we started a contemporary service at 8:30 a.m. and kept the traditional service very traditional. It took little time for the early service to outgrow the late service. There were calls from the young crowd to switch the order of the two services. Our music director, who had grown increasingly unhappy with the situation, resigned. My approval rating with the older set sank faster than a concrete canoe. Another colleague left to plant a church. Tension mounted. We had a congregational meeting in which I shared our vision for worship and let people voice their frustrations. One lady criticized me for playing a guitar in the worship service. A man said we were abandoning "true worship." A young father stood to defend the new contemporary direction. One after another, unhappy people rose to give impassioned speeches. It was plain we were a church divided.

The elders and I knew a compromise had to be struck. We decided to have just one blended worship service. If the two sides can't get along, we'll get everyone together in the same room and make *everyone* miserable. And that's exactly what happened.

Eventually I had elders telling me it was time for me to go. Gossip was everywhere. Someone told me what a poor leader I was. Another man told me I was unfit to be a senior pastor. I got anonymous notes and emails of complaint. They all started with words like, "I'm concerned . . ." Giving plummeted. I was crushed. My capital was all gone. It was clearly time to get out of there. But where would I go? What would I do?

One morning I wrote seven words in my journal: "It wasn't supposed to be this way." I had become a minister of the gospel because I loved Jesus and the Word. I loved administering the sacraments, equipping the saints, shepherding the flock, and helping people grow. Instead of being a pastor, it felt like I was a referee at a Stanley Cup final—or, more accurately, the puck.

I wish I could say that none of this was my fault. I wish I could tell you I responded to all these crises with the meekness of Moses, the steadiness of Joshua, the wisdom of Solomon, the prayerful spirit of Nehemiah, the courage of Paul, and the love of Christ. But

"It Wasn't Supposed to Be This Way"

I can't. The truth is, I was part of the problem at New Life Church. I went into that church naïve and unprepared. I should have listened to my wife. I should have asked more questions before accepting the call. I should have taken more time to build trust. I should have been more careful about introducing change. When Hurricane Worship Wars hit, I should have been more prayerful, less of a pushover, more loving, patient, and honest. The conflict eventually exploded in a "splant" (that's a split disguised as a church plant) that hurt many people, including my family and me. It threatened to end my career as a pastor and seriously damage my marriage.

But through that catastrophe, I learned valuable lessons. By God's grace I moved on, recovered a love for the church, and eventually assumed the role of lead pastor elsewhere.

In the chapters that follow I will reflect on my experience and share the lessons learned. My goal, if you will walk with me, is to help you recognize the signs of an impending catastrophe, limit its damage, learn from it, and live with gospel optimism for the future.

Let's begin with seven words you should commit to memory.

Chapter 2
It *Is* Supposed to Be This Way

"Tony, you're a liar. You're going to have to leave the church."

Pastor Tony heard the words, but they made no sense. It felt like he'd just been tackled by a 300-lb. linebacker—speared, more like it—and hammered into the ground. The eyes of six deacons seated grimly around the conference table stared blankly at their pastor. Tony gulped and said, "Excuse me?"

"You have a pattern of deception in your life, Tony," said the chairman of the deacon board. "You're a liar. You'll need to resign."

Tony Kendall had been at Bayside Baptist Church for just three years. The church had embraced Tony and his wife Emily with enthusiasm. They loved Pastor Tony's passion in the pulpit and his knack at connecting Scripture with life. He had hit the ground running. He got the staff pulling in the same direction and sparked renewed vision among the people for blessing the city.

But before long, Tony knew there were problems at Bayside Baptist. In fact, the first sign of an approaching storm appeared the first week he was there. One of the trustees of the church took Tony out to lunch and told him the deacons and trustees weren't on speaking terms. Tony was shocked. This had certainly not come up in the interview process. How could the spiritual leaders of the church allow such a thing?

When the deacons asked Tony to start a contemporary worship service, Tony accepted the challenge but warned them it

It Is Supposed to Be This Way

would not be easy. And Tony was right. It was not easy. Beliefs about worship are about as hard to change as a Long Islander's accent. But as it turned out, the contemporary worship service was the least of Tony's problems.

Tony butted heads often with Bayside's assistant pastor, Matt Rhodes. Matt knew he was on the way out, and made plans to start a church elsewhere in the community. But he would not go quietly. Matt had an ally on the deacon board named Steve Boyd, who was also the board chairman. Matt had often run to Steve whenever he didn't like something Tony had done or said. Now Matt told Steve the content of his latest conversation with Tony. He had even recorded the conversation and sent Steve a copy. So several weeks later, at the next board meeting, Steve asked Tony about something he had told Matt.

"Did you say that or not?"

Tony honestly couldn't remember. The conversation was several weeks old. "No, I don't think so. I certainly don't remember it."

Steve slammed his fists on the conference table. "Tony, you're a liar." He pulled his iPhone out of his pocket and played the recorded conversation for all to hear.

"Well, I guess you're right. I did say that."

Steve said, "You're going to have to leave the church, Tony. There's a pattern of deception in your life. You can either resign now or we're going to vote to kick you out of the church."

Tony was speechless. Yes, he was wrong. He didn't have his facts straight about a conversation with his assistant pastor. But did this rise to the level of an irreparable breach of trust, a sin that merited dismissal?

What Tony knew that the other deacons sitting around the table that night did not, was that Steve had had a long-running dislike for Tony. He didn't care for Tony's preaching. He questioned Tony's motives for ministry. Whenever Tony looked at Steve from the pulpit, Steve would scowl back at him. Matt, the assistant pastor, had totally convinced Steve that Tony Kendall was a fraud.

Tony knew it was over. He could fight to stay at Bayside, but Steve held all the cards. Tony slumped in his chair and said hardly

9

a word the rest of the meeting. His brain was pounding with questions. "What will I do? Where will I go? What will I tell Emily and the kids? How will we sell our home? It's underwater. How can this be happening?"

As he started his car and pulled out of the church parking lot, Tony knew many tears would fall in the Kendall home that night.

Let's start with something very basic to pastoral ministry: It *is* supposed to be this way. Believing those seven words and rehearsing them often is an essential part of crisis preparation.

To be a pastor is to be called by Jesus into conflict. As one church leader put it, "Being a pastor is like death by a thousand paper cuts."[1] The great evangelist Alan Redpath once said, "If you're a Christian pastor, you're always in a crisis—either in the middle of one, coming out of one, or going into one."[2] It may be unjust, and it won't be this way after Jesus comes back, but right now, storms of controversy, rejection, discord, betrayal, and opposition are inevitable. They are part of shepherding broken people in a broken world out of your own broken condition.

The Puritan Richard Baxter (1615–1691) pastored a church in Kidderminster, England, for close to twenty years. He wrote in his journal one day, ". . . the more I do, the more hatred and trouble I draw upon me." Jonathan Edwards (1703–1758) said in his farewell sermon to his Northampton congregation, "It often comes to pass in this evil world, that great differences and controversies arise between ministers and the people under their pastoral care."[3] Now make no mistake, some pastors bring hatred and trouble upon themselves. They preach or lead poorly, or fall into sin and bring disgrace upon their own and their Savior's name. But Scripture, history, and experience all agree that a faithful minister will sooner or later find himself in the eye of a hurricane.

1. Asghar, "Ranking the 9 Toughest Leadership Roles," lines 27–28.
2. Shelley, *Well-Intentioned Dragons*, 135.
3. Edwards, "Farewell Sermon," ccii.

It Is Supposed to Be This Way

You've heard God will not give you more than you can handle? That's a lie. God *will* give you more than you can handle. Just read the book of Psalms.

The Bible is full of examples of spiritual leaders who suffered. The apostle Paul said to the Corinthians who questioned his credentials,

> Five times I received at the hands of the Jews the forty lashes less one. Three times I was beaten with rods. Once I was stoned. Three times I was shipwrecked; a night and a day I was adrift at sea; on frequent journeys, in danger from rivers, danger from robbers, danger from my own people, danger from Gentiles, danger in the city, danger in the wilderness, danger at sea, danger from false brothers; in toil and hardship, through many a sleepless night, in hunger and thirst, often without food, in cold and exposure. And, apart from other things, there is the daily pressure on me of my anxiety for all the churches (2 Cor 11:24–28).

Speaking for all ministers everywhere Paul writes, "We are afflicted in every way . . . perplexed . . . persecuted . . . struck down . . . always carrying in the body the death of Jesus" (2 Cor 4:8–10). Don't let Paul's qualifiers ("not crushed," "not driven to despair," "not forsaken," and "not destroyed") diminish the impact of the troubles Paul says we are due.

The Old Testament prophets were rarely, if ever, the objects of people's favor. Jesus once lamented, "O Jerusalem, Jerusalem, the city that kills the prophets and stones those who are sent to it!" (Matt 23:37). Not without reason is Jeremiah called the Weeping Prophet. He mourned the sad state of affairs in his homeland of Judah. He pleaded with his people to return to the Lord who loved them with an everlasting love (Jer 31:3). He was faithful to his calling "to pluck up and to break down, to destroy and to overthrow, to build and to plant" (Jer 1:10). What did Jeremiah get in return? Trouble. "Let us strike him with the tongue, and let us not pay attention to any of his words," the people said (Jer 18:18). They called Jeremiah a traitor, beat him, put him in the stocks, confined him in a dungeon, threw him into a cistern and left him to die, and finally carried him off to Egypt where, according to one tradition, he was stoned to death. I've often wondered what a modern-day preacher of health, wealth, and prosperity would say to Jeremiah.

About the prophets the author of Hebrews tells us,

> Some were tortured, refusing to accept release . . . Others suffered mocking and flogging, and even chains and imprisonment. They were stoned, they were sawn in two, they were killed with the sword. They went about in skins of sheep and goats, destitute, afflicted, mistreated—of whom the world was not worthy—wandering about in deserts and mountains, and in dens and caves of the earth (Heb 11:35–38).

Comparing the Old Testament prophets to twenty-first-century pastors may be a little like comparing the Atlantic Ocean to the retention pond in my backyard. But the pastoral call today has much in common with God's call to the ancient prophets. We labor for the same things they did: the reign of God, pure worship, true repentance, faith in the covenant promises, dependence on a Redeemer, obedience to God's Word, love to fellow believers, mercy and justice toward the oppressed. When pastors faithfully fulfill their prophetic calling they may not be thrown into a cistern but they will experience "the raging wind and tempest" (Ps 55:8).

"We were . . . promised sufferings. They were part of the program," wrote C. S. Lewis in *A Grief Observed*.[4] Every pastor I know who has been in ministry for some time has been hit by waves of trouble, both from without and within. Peter Drucker once said that the job of a pastor is one of the four hardest in America.[5] (The other three were the CEO of a hospital, a university president, and the President of the United States.) I've heard ministers of the gospel compared to lightning rods that attract the complaints and grievances of church members. As one pastor put it, "The only pastors who don't experience regular, character-building periods

---

4. Lewis, *Grief Observed*, 53.
5. Wagner, "The Secret Pain of Pastors," lines 1–8.

It Is Supposed to Be This Way

of conflict, are either bullies who walk all over everyone or cowards afraid to stand up for what God wants to accomplish."[6]

If the statistics floating around the Internet are even partially true, they highlight the fact that the work of a pastor is complex and demanding—more so than people in the pew realize. Pastoral ministry is taking a greater toll on pastors and their families than ever before. A contributing factor is the sharply decreased respectability of the pastoral vocation in the United States today. But what Pastor Tony and a million other pastors need to realize is that church hurricanes—fights, controversies, divisions, misunderstandings, and the like—don't just materialize out of a vacuum. The pastor is on the front lines of a spiritual battle that has raged ever since Adam and Eve were kicked out of Eden and will continue until the return of the second Adam. This is the battle that Paul says we fight, not "against flesh and blood, but against the rulers, against the authorities, against the cosmic powers over this present darkness, against the spiritual forces of evil in the heavenly places" (Eph 6:12).

I am not excusing pastors and congregations from culpability when things go haywire in the church. Church leaders and their followers often do stupid, sinful things and must bear the consequences of their mistakes. But behind every storm that disrupts the peace and purity of a local church, our enemy the Devil, who "prowls around like a roaring lion" (1 Pet 5:8), seeks to devour the pastor and the flock that follows him or her.

In his book *Dangerous Calling* Paul David Tripp writes,

> Why do so many pastors report being over-burdened and over-stressed? Why do so many pastors report tension between family life and ministry life? Why does pastoral ministry often seem like more of a trial than a joy? Why is there often disharmony between the private life of the pastor and his public ministry persona? Why are there often dysfunctional relationships between the pastor and his ministry leaders or staff? Why is the ministry life of many pastors shockingly short? Perhaps we have

---

6. Rowell, "Introduction," 9.

Part 1: Crisis Readiness

forgotten that *pastoral ministry is war* and that you will never live successfully in the pastorate if you live with a peacetime mentality.[7] (emphasis mine)

Pastoral ministry is war. That's why I'm arguing it *is* supposed to be this way. Pastoring a church is supposed to be hard, and disorienting, and chaotic, and lonely, and insuperable. It's more than that, thankfully, but it is not less. I once saw a book in a Christian bookstore titled *Mastering the Pastoral Role* and had to grin. The authors meant well I'm sure, but the pastoral role can no more be "mastered" than can a hurricane churning through the Gulf of Mexico.

In *Pilgrim's Progress* (a far better read than many of the books aimed at pastors these days), John Bunyan pictures Christian, having left the sweet safety of the House Beautiful, engaging the "foul fiend" Apollyon in hand-to-hand combat in the Valley of Humiliation. Apollyon is the Devil himself, the embodiment of all that is evil and opposed to God. Apollyon is "hideous to behold." Instead of immediately dispatching Christian with fireballs, Apollyon tries to wear him down with psychological tactics. He peppers the pilgrim with questions: Where are you from? Where are you going? Why have you run away from your king? What makes you think your king will reward you? Then Apollyon brings up Christian's mistakes and failures. Listen to his disdainful accusations:

> Very soon after leaving the City of Destruction, you were quickly discouraged when you almost drowned in the Slough of Despond. You made several wrong attempts to be rid of your burden, whereas you should have waited until your Prince relieved you of it himself. Through shameful over-sleeping, you lost a very precious personal possession; also you were nearly persuaded to turn back at the sight of those fierce lions; and when you converse, as you travel, of what you have heard and seen, your inward desire is for personal glory with regard to everything that you say or do.[8]

7. Tripp, *Dangerous Calling*, 97–98.
8. Bunyan and Horner, *Pilgrim's Progress*, 73–74.

It Is Supposed to Be This Way

Such is the voice of the Accuser. A faithful pastor hears this voice often. It reminds him of all his "nots": duties not done, prayers not prayed, family devotions not led, the sick not visited, the strays not sought, sermons not preached well or preached with impure motives. This accusing voice seeks to weaken confidence and work loose the bond between pastor and gospel.

But Apollyon is not content with mere dialogue with Christian. He throws darts at him ("thick as hail," says Bunyan) and wounds him in his head, hand, and foot. Pastors—and their family members—are frequently the targets of unkind remarks, characterizations, and labels. I was once rebuked publicly during a worship service for saying in my sermon that God has a sense of humor. (I must say I still find Acts 20:7–12, among other things, a funny story.) I've been slandered by church members whom I had welcomed into the church and discipled. I've lost count of the number of dangerous people who've threatened me because I called the cops on them. I've been patronized, ignored, gossiped about, lectured, avoided, misunderstood, unfriended on Facebook, falsely accused, voted against, insulted, walked out on, and blindsided. And sometimes I didn't even deserve it.

I'm not trying to win sympathy. Nor do I dare compare my light and momentary troubles to the sufferings of Christians throughout history and at the present time for whom affiliation with Jesus means more costly persecution, torture, and even death. I'm simply repeating what Jesus said: "In the world you will have tribulation" (John 16:33).

With the help of God and the sword of the Spirit, Christian goes on to defeat Apollyon. But no sooner is he out of the Valley of Humiliation than he enters the Valley of the Shadow of Death. Bunyan's whole point in *Pilgrim's Progress* is to make sure we understand that the journey to glory is hazardous and exhausting. There are seasons of rest and favor, to be sure, but they are scarce. Jesus described the life of the Christian as one of self-denial and cross-carrying (Luke 9:23). If such is the norm for disciples in general, how much more should it be the norm for pastors, whose example disciples are to follow (Heb 13:7, 1 Pet 5:3)

Lanier Ivester writes, "We're miners, really, we servants of the true King, plunging through a darkened world in enemy territory to retrieve the scattered bits of Eden that were made to flame in the light of the sun."[9] No wonder, then, that the pastoral call is a call to suffer. It's supposed to be that way. Therefore, crisis preparation requires a realistic, humble, watchful attitude. A pastor dare not go to the field with self-assured naïveté or the carefree hubris of a know-it-all. "When pride comes, then comes disgrace," wrote Solomon, "but with the humble is wisdom" (Prov 11:2).

Don't be surprised by a ministry hurricane. Expect it, and it will be far less likely to blow you, your family, and your church away.

---

9. Ivester, "The Two Trees," lines 84–85.

Chapter 3
Know Your Church

"THERE IS NOT A church in America that I would pastor for $5 million. I would manage a Wendy's before I'd be the senior pastor of a church. I'm a recovering senior pastor, just like a recovering alcoholic. And I'm just not going to take the first drink again. I have zero ambition for the role."

Meet Pastor Robert. In the mid-1990s, Robert was flourishing in his role as an associate pastor of administration. He taught a Sunday school class of 200 people. He was leading several strategic ministry teams and had lots of influence in the church. "But," he says, "something in me itched for the senior pastor role." So Robert accepted a call to a large, 1,200-member church in another state.

Unfortunately, the pastor search committee of this congregation painted a too-rosy picture of the church. They even concealed from him the church's firm belief in baptismal succession.

Nevertheless, Robert describes his first two years at the church as a "honeymoon." People were responding to the gospel. The church purchased land for expansion. But then Robert made his first mistake: he invited a guest speaker from a different denomination to preach one Sunday. "Never do that again," he was told by the church officers. Robert agreed. But soon he made another big mistake: he allowed a couple to join the church who had not, according to fellow leaders, been properly baptized. Church leaders were incensed.

Part 1: Crisis Readiness

Robert believed the time had come for a showdown. According to him, power brokers in the church held narrow, unbiblical views of baptism and the Lord's Supper. So Robert called a congregational meeting. He wanted to put it to a vote: Was he correct about the ordinances, or were his fellow church leaders correct? The day of the congregational meeting, people came out of the woodwork. "It was the blackest Sunday morning of my life," Robert recalls. The news media set up cameras on the sidewalk. People who hadn't attended the church for years showed up to cast their vote. The meeting got out of control. People were shouting at each other. When the votes were counted, Robert's view prevailed, but by just over fifty percent.

The church split down the middle. The "losers" left and started a new church. The "winners" stayed, but now the church was half as big as before. The congregation couldn't sustain their budget. Staff members had to be released. Robert's standing in the community had taken a big hit. "Pastor Robert is mean and graceless," people said. Robert's marriage suffered too. He and his wife were hardly speaking. Worse, Robert's enemies spread rumors about his wife. In Robert's words, "She was accused of horrible, personal things that couldn't be true of her—vile things. They said she was visiting 'unsavory places.' Someone nailed a dead woodchuck to the front door of our house. It was a nightmare."

Fortunately, Robert found his way to another church many miles away and was hired as an assistant pastor. But, he says, he'll never itch for the senior pastor role again. "I love my comparative anonymity. I can go to Walmart in shorts and a T-shirt and nobody knows who I am."

As Robert told me his story, I felt sad. Here was a man who went to his new call with a genuine desire to see the gospel flourish in his community. He had a healthy catholic spirit. Augustine's maxim—"In essentials, unity; in nonessentials, liberty; in all things, charity"—summed up his philosophy of ministry. Now he says you couldn't pay him enough money to be a senior pastor again. What happened?

What happened is a ministry hurricane, a tempest of secrecy and division that ripped a congregation in half and ground up an unsuspecting pastor and his family. Robert is not above blame. He admits that his "itch" for the senior pastor role was driven, at least in part, by a desire for personal glory. And calling a congregational meeting in order to have a showdown was most unwise. But Pastor Robert's story illustrates the fact that in many churches, a catastrophe is just waiting to happen. All it takes is a new leader who has either not done his homework or not been told the church's real story. Or both.

Every church has a story. Its past is dotted with ups and downs, successes and failures, home runs and strikeouts. Every church has its own set of non-negotiables, its own pet doctrines, spirituality tests, rules for who's "in" and who's "out," motivations and values. They are not written down anywhere. Church members, even leaders, may not be able to articulate them. But violate them, and like Pastor Robert you will likely wind up in the eye of a hurricane. That's why it's critical to take your time and do your research before accepting a call to a church. You must hunt for the church's unique story like Indiana Jones searching for the Holy Grail. Once you have found it, you must listen to it over and over.

I know what I'm talking about. As you'll recall from chapter 1, I accepted a call to a large congregation after seven years of blessed ministry at a smaller church. In retrospect, I was bedazzled by the size of New Life Church, the increase in salary, and the prestige of leading a flagship church in my denomination. My ambition blinded me to several realities that anyone else could have easily seen. The church had had just two senior pastors in its twenty-year history—each a charismatic leader. Both men were gifted but authoritarian and polarizing figures. When I arrived on the scene, there were camps of staunch admirers and outspoken detractors of each pastor. The damage each of these leaders had done to the church was immense. The founding pastor's ten-year "my way or the highway" approach to ministry alienated leaders and members

Part 1: Crisis Readiness

alike and caused his eventual dismissal. The pastor who followed him—my predecessor—had an adulterous affair with a woman in the church and was deposed from the ministry. The affair led to a lawsuit. Attorneys for all sides got involved. Details about the case had to be kept secret. Church members were upset about the way things were handled. Some left. Those who stayed were confused, angry, heartbroken, bitter—or all of the above.

So for twenty years New Life Church had suffered abuse by powerful but faulty leaders. It was a clear shepherding opportunity. The elders of the church should have created an environment in which members could express their pain, vent, ask questions, and begin to heal. But unfortunately, the elders circled the wagons around themselves. In the name of safeguarding the flock, they hid facts from the people and met behind closed doors. A rift of mistrust developed between the sheep and their shepherds.

Despite these warning signs, when I heard about the opening at New Life I submitted my résumé and was invited to interview. Unlike New Life's previous pastors, my leadership style is relational, not authoritarian. I am strong in the shepherding-preaching-teaching department, but weaker in the vision-casting, organizational leadership department. I made this clear in the interviews. In fact, I talked a lot about myself—but did a poor job of fact-finding about New Life Church. I did not call either of the two previous pastors. I did not bother to talk to neighbors around the church. I did not contact disaffected church members, or hurt staff members, or pastors of other churches in town. I lobbed softball questions at the pastor search committee. I ignored the cautions of people who cared about me. I assumed that if I got the job, preached the gospel, and loved people, all would be well.

Needless to say, I was extremely naïve. I was offered the position of senior pastor of New Life Church and took it. And from the day I arrived until the day I left five years later, one storm after another pummeled the church and wore me out.

Did God call me to New Life Church? Yes. I believe in the sovereignty of God and trust this was all part of his plan. But I had

Know Your Church

made a big mistake: I went there without knowing the church's story.

Some of you reading this book are considering a call to a church. Others are in the early months of your pastorate. The reason it's important to know your church is that ministry hurricanes don't happen in a vacuum. Storm clouds gather in the distance long before they do their damage. If you listen carefully to a church's story, you can hear the sound of approaching winds. Failing to listen spells Trouble. Even if you've been leading your church for some time, it's never too late to get to know your church's story more completely.

I'm reminded of what happened to Galveston, Texas, on September 8, 1900. The Galveston Hurricane remains the deadliest natural disaster in US history. Estimates of the number of dead range between 8,000 and 12,000. Storm prediction was in its infancy at the time. All the National Weather Service could say was that a tropical storm was on its way to the United States from Cuba. It could have hit Florida and moved out into the Atlantic, for all they knew. Galveston had no seawall. City officials claimed one was not necessary. Consequently, few people were alarmed when rain clouds began rolling in mid-morning and wind started to pick up. By the end of the day the "Great Storm," as it came to be called, was a Category 4 hurricane accompanied by nine inches of rain and a sixteen-foot storm surge. Its maximum winds were estimated at 140 miles per hour. The dead were so numerous bodies were piled up on the beach and burned.

Modern technology gives us an advantage the people of Galveston didn't have at the turn of the twentieth century. Today's meteorologists can predict the path and power of hurricanes with amazing accuracy. But when it comes to predicting church hurricanes, we're more like the people of Galveston in 1900. There are no instruments that can spot a church split or dissension in the making. But the warning signs are there. Let me mention five:

Part 1: Crisis Readiness

1. *Lack of a clear vision.* In a healthy church, there is a clear sense of calling and purpose. The members and leaders alike can tell you why their church exists. They may express it in slightly different words, but in the main they agree: "We exist to make disciples of all nations." "Our church is about making a difference in this community." "We want to know Jesus and make him known." If, on the other hand, you ask ten different people what their church is about, and you hear five, eight, or ten different things, you can expect a storm sooner or later. We'll talk more about vision in chapter 6.

2. *Inward rather than outward focus.* In a healthy church, members want to bless the people around them. They understand that the promise God gave Abraham—"in you all the families of the earth shall be blessed" (Gen 12:3)—applies to the church today. They are willing to sacrifice their time, talents, and treasure for the gospel's advance in the world. More important to them than the color of the carpet in the sanctuary, the style of worship, the eloquence of the preacher, and the size of the church playground is faithfulness to the Great Commission: "Go therefore and make disciples of all nations" (Matt 28:19). If, on the other hand, you hear the majority of church members talking about the things they want in their church in order to be comfortable and happy, expect a storm any day.

3. *Worship of the past.* In a healthy church, people celebrate the past but are living with present realities and optimism about the future. Its charter members are given the honor they are due but are not coddled. Previous pastors are remembered with gratitude but not revered. Members feel that the best days of the church are yet to come. If, on the other hand, the constant refrain is how wonderful things used to be "when Pastor So-and-So was here," when everyone sang hymns from the hymnal, or when the church was debt free, you may want to start hurricane-proofing your heart.

4. *Neglect of the means of grace.* In a healthy church, members steadily engage in the ordinary means of grace: the Word of God, prayer, fellowship, and the sacraments of baptism and the Lord's Supper. Like the early Christians, they "[devote] themselves to the apostles' teaching and the fellowship, to the breaking of bread and the prayers" (Acts 2:42). They look forward to gathering for corporate worship on the Lord's Day and in homes throughout the week. If, on the other hand, church members are content with a shallow commitment to God's book and Christ's body, storm clouds will gather as you lead in a Godward direction.

5. *Lack of love and graciousness.* In a healthy church, people seek to build one another up and meet each other's needs. They know how well God has loved them and want to "pay it forward." They practice hospitality and invite newcomers into their small group gatherings. When someone sins against another, he or she repents and is forgiven. The job of caring for the sick, bereaved, poor, and lonely is not left to the staff and officers but is the shared responsibility of the congregation. Members understand the difference between open-hand and closed-hand doctrines. They give grace to those with a different point of view. If, however, you detect a hardened spirit of pride, legalism, narrow-mindedness, or longstanding grudges among the membership, get ready; a hurricane may be on the horizon.

If three or more of those warning signs are present in a church and you do nothing about them, that church may simply die a slow, quiet death. But if you step up and call congregants to a missional vision, an outward focus, a future perspective, commitment to biblical and theological maturity, and humble love, don't be surprised when the storm clouds that have been forming in the distance hit landfall. And you'll be the one people blame. Learning a church's story takes time and effort, but the investment will pay off. Whether you are considering a new call or are already on board, the better you know the church the less likely you will be to sink should a ministry hurricane come ashore.

How can you get to know a church's story? Here are eight suggestions:

1. *If you are considering a call to a church, before you accept it interview the interviewers.* Floating around the Internet, there are great sets of questions to ask a search committee. Ask them everything, including: What is this church's mission or purpose? What is the pastoral history of the church? Why did each pastor leave? What were those pastors' best contributions and worst mistakes? What does this church believe about politics, abortion, homosexuality, unmarried couples living together, the role of women in ministry, homeschooling, divorce and remarriage, consumer debt, tithing, worship music, charismatic gifts, use of alcohol, discipline of children, and race relations? How do the leaders of this church view church debt? What are this church's goals? Where is the pastor's job description? Does this church have a constitution, and do you follow it? What are you looking for in a leader? What leadership mistakes are you hoping to correct with this hire? How many people have become Christians through this church in the past year? What are the main needs of this community? What has this church been doing to meet those needs? What would you like to see improved? What church programs are most and least effective? Why have people left this church? What do you expect from a pastor's spouse? What are this church's strengths and weaknesses? When you dream about the future of this church, what do you see?

2. *Meet with the governing board of the church.* Ask them the same questions as listed above. Note any disparities between their responses and those of the search committee.

3. *Talk to others in the community about the church.* Walk door to door around the church and ask neighbors, "What do you think about this church?" Meet with pastors of other area congregations. Find out what's on their hearts for the

community. What are their priorities? How do they view your church? Are they open to having a relationship with you and your church? Meet several civic and government leaders and school principals and ask them the same questions.

4. *Get a demographic study of the community.* The website of the US Small Business Administration (www.sba.gov) is a valuable tool. The Association of Religion Data Archives (http://www.thearda.com/DemographicMap) is a free resource for mapping your community and discovering a wealth of relevant census data.

5. *If you would be relocating, spend a week in the community.* Read local newspapers. Visit the schools. Walk Main Street or the shopping malls. Eat at local diners and engage people in conversation. Get to know your way around. Listen carefully to your family members' assessment.

6. *Talk to previous pastors.* Ask them about their experience with the church. What do they celebrate? What do they regret? What would they do differently if they could lead that church again? Who are the people that may cause you problems?

7. *Attend a worship service of the church as a "secret shopper."* Sit in the back and observe. How well were you welcomed? What do you see in the members' interaction with each other and with guests? How engaged in worship is the congregation? How clearly is the gospel articulated and celebrated? How would you characterize the mood of the service? How quickly do the people exit after the service? Listen to their conversations with each other; what are they talking about? Did anyone speak to you after the service?

8. *Interview random church members.* Call a group of ten or more people listed in the membership directory. Ask these members to share their experience, good and bad, about the church. Has the church helped them grow spiritually? If so, how? If not, why not? What are the church's strengths and weaknesses? How are they personally involved in the church?

PART 1: CRISIS READINESS

What concerns, if any, do they have about the church? Can they articulate the church's purpose and goals?

Now that we've talked about your church's story, it's time for an even more important subject: *your* story.

Chapter 4
Know Yourself

IN THE LAST CHAPTER I emphasized the importance of understanding the story of a church. As imperative as that is, it pales in comparison to understanding your own story. In his book *Leading with a Limp*, Dan Allender writes,

> . . . in order to better comprehend the story of God, a leader must first enter into his own story. Since you were there when your story happened, entering it would seem like the easiest thing in the world to do, but actually nothing is more difficult. The reason is we only know—or let ourselves know—part of our story. We hold on either to what we wish to remember or to what serves us well to recall, and we flee from the parts of our story that most deeply expose and unnerve us.[1]

Allender is saying the same thing John Calvin wrote in the opening sentence of his *Institutes of the Christian Religion*: "The whole sum of our wisdom—wisdom, that is, which deserves to be called true and assured—broadly consists of two parts, knowledge of God and knowledge of ourselves."[2] Knowing God and knowing yourself are inseparable. The more you grasp your desperate need of salvation revealed in your story (including those things that "deeply expose and unnerve" you), the more fully you

---

1. Allender, *Leading with a Limp*, 161.
2. Calvin, *Institutes*, 1.

will know God and *get* the gospel. And the more "the light of the knowledge of the glory of God in the face of Jesus Christ" (2 Cor 4:6) shines upon your heart, the more fully you will understand your story. There is no true knowledge of God without knowledge of self, and there is no true knowledge of self apart from the knowledge of God.

Is this just so much psychobabble—all this talk about story and self-knowledge? Not at all. When I was in seminary, my mentor, the late Seth Dyrness, told me something I've never forgotten: *You minister out of who you are.* Seven more valuable words have never been spoken for pastors. If you don't know who you are—if you don't know your story—you'll forever be trying to root your identity and security in things like ministry success, wealth, reputation, the love and approval of others, physical fitness, and so on. Ministry is exceedingly difficult for men and women who don't know who they are. Too many people in your church are willing to define ministry for you, and no two of them agree. Pastoral survival requires self-knowledge.

In the Bible, King Saul strikes me as a man who did not know himself—and paid for it dearly. The son of Kish the Benjaminite, Saul was "a handsome young man. There was not a man among the people of Israel more handsome than he" (1 Sam 9:2). Though chosen by God and hailed enthusiastically by the Israelites as their first king, Saul's true colors soon revealed themselves. On two key occasions (1 Sam 13 and 15), Saul failed to trust and obey the word of God delivered through the prophet Samuel. As a result, God took the throne away from Saul and gave it to David, the man after God's heart. The final years of Saul's reign show just how insecure, jealous, and cruel he could be. He could not endure being known as the king who killed thousands while David killed ten thousands. He even tried to murder his own son Jonathan.

What was Saul's problem? It seems he was all about appearances. Read through the biblical narrative about King Saul and you'll see much about his strength and physical features but little about his heart. "And when he stood among the people, he was taller than any of the people from his shoulders upward. And Samuel said to all the people, 'Do you see him whom the Lord has chosen? There is none like him among all the people.' And all the people shouted, 'Long live the king!'" (1 Sam 10:23-24). While David, like Saul, was strong and handsome—not to mention far from perfect—both the biblical narrative and the book of Psalms reveal that he had a humble and whole heart. It was because "the Lord looks on the heart," not the outward appearance, that God directed Samuel to anoint David as Saul's successor (1 Sam 16:6-13).

Saul found his identity in outward things. As anyone knows, outward things tend to change, break down, age, and eventually perish. Basing your identity on things so slippery and ephemeral produces a disintegrated personality. Disintegrated people are inconsistent. They make decisions on the basis of what others think rather than what is right or wise—like Saul's decision to sacrifice the burnt offering instead of waiting for Samuel. Disintegrated people are tossed here and there by the winds of circumstances, emotions, the latest fads, and the wants and needs of other people rather than being rooted in core convictions. Integrated people, on the other hand, think and behave in ways consistent with who they really are. (The word "integrity" comes from this concept of being together, undivided, or consistent.) They live by those famous words of Polonius in *Hamlet*: "To thine own self be true; / And it must follow, as the night the day, / Thou canst not then be false to any man."[3]

Pastors, more than any other single group of professionals, are susceptible to the Saul Syndrome. We like helping people grow, meeting people's needs. That's fine. But most of us are "approval sucks," to quote the late John Miller, founder of World Harvest Mission. As I write this sentence, according to a Rasmussen poll the approval rating of our chief executive stands at forty-five percent. And he's still standing? My goodness, I would be devastated if my approval rating as a pastor was anything below ninety. I like to be liked. And if I'm not constantly repenting and believing the gospel, that desire to be liked will become my Golden Calf.

3. Shakespeare, *Hamlet*, Act 1, Scene 3.

Part 1: Crisis Readiness

How can you avoid the Saul Syndrome? It begins with knowing your story.

I grew up in the Bible Belt—that swath of the southern United States where most people go to church (or believe they should) and where in order to have assurance of salvation you don't smoke, or chew, or go with girls who do. At least that's the way things were back when *The Andy Griffith Show* and the Beatles and the bouffant hairdo were all the rage. Mom and Dad made sure we were at First Presbyterian Church every Sunday. Why, we even went to church when we were on vacation. They modeled good morals, taught good manners, and drilled into my brother and me a solid work ethic. The words "I love you" were seldom spoken. But I sure remember "Sit up straight." "Eat with your mouth closed." "Have you done your homework?" "Did you finish mowing the lawn?" and "Let's see that report card." Mom and Dad saw themselves as providers, and they were good at it. Both had grown up in harsher times and in what we today would call dysfunctional families. Dad had served in the army in World War II. He lost his brother Jack to a German sniper's bullet. Mom's alcoholic father abandoned the family when she was but five. What parenting skills my folks had were honed in the school of hard knocks and from the pages of Dr. Spock's *Baby and Child Care* instead of the more child-centric *Focus on the Family* broadcasts of the 1970s and '80s. Consequently, love was written between the lines. If it was affirmation I wanted, I knew what to do: Excel. Be outstanding. Make all As—better yet, A-pluses. Run for student body president and win. Star in the school play. Score the winning touchdown. Impress Dad's business associates. Go the extra mile. Visit the old lady down the street. Give the graduation speech. Keep my weight under control. Don't go to extremes. Don't be a jerk. Stay out of trouble.

And stay out of trouble I did. I didn't smoke, or chew, or go with girls who did. In fact, I did none of the things teenagers are generally famous for, such as being a smart ass, drinking, smoking pot, getting pulled over for speeding, flunking algebra, or any other such nonsense. *I was a good boy.*

Problem is, as you hopefully found out a long time ago, no one is really good. I may have cleaned the outside of the plate and cup, but inside I was full of dead men's bones (Matt 23:25–28). Since home was not a safe place to share my fears, insecurities, and questions, I stuffed all those things. I became a very good "stuffer." I spent lots of time alone as an adolescent. I felt horribly inferior to most other boys, especially the strong ones. I discovered the tantalizing world of *Playboy* magazine and spent hours and hours creating a private, sexy persona. I found out I could be a pretty good liar, and I often cheated in school. I learned how to put on a smile and an act. Outwardly I came off as a smart, self-assured, nice person. Inwardly I was racked with doubts about my looks, my masculinity, and my competence. I was petrified of failing. Failure would have been a total embarrassment to both my parents and me. School dances were the death of me. I felt like a complete idiot.

But no one would have guessed all this. I was a chameleon. I could be funny and sociable with my church friends, highly intellectual with my scholarly friends, and tough around my football friends. But when I went into my room and closed the door, I was one scared, lonely, ashamed little boy.

In his song "The Day I Gave My Heart Away," Billy Crockett sings about a little boy like me:

> A child grows up and learns to hide to keep his heart together
> From early on he tries to mold a face that lasts forever
> A pair of eyes that let the boy look out but won't let you look in
> He is collecting words that he can use so he can always win
> A frightened heart that stays at home, that smiles a lot but lives alone
> A little boy with grown-up ways afraid to give his heart away.
> That little boy with man-size greed who held his heart so tight
> Was sure that if he let it go he'd lose it overnight
> So there he was in his own world, the one he built himself

PART 1: CRISIS READINESS

> Made sure the doors were locked, the curtains drawn, his heart up on the shelf
> A frightened heart that stays at home, that smiles a lot but lives alone
> A little boy with grown-up ways afraid to give his heart away.[4]

I was that little boy with a frightened heart. Even now, as a sixty-something who has managed to stay married, raise four healthy children, and serve four churches as an acceptably competent pastor, it's painful to revisit that lonely, locked bedroom in my mind. I don't want to feel again how much I hated the big breasts on my adolescent body and dreaded going to the beach or the swimming pool with friends who looked "normal." I don't want to recall how I felt at that Rotary Club banquet when I, a naïve high-school junior, gave a speech and totally botched it in front of my Dad and all his friends. I don't want to remember that weekend trip with my high-school girlfriend—yes, the girl I adored and thought I'd marry one day—when she broke up with me and left me looking like an absolute jerk. I don't want to recall how angry I got at my little baby Rebecca when she was just a few weeks old and had colic so bad she cried all day and all night long for weeks. I don't want to relive the arguments with my wife when the scared little boy inside of me donned the skin of an authoritarian know-it-all. I don't want to resuscitate those years of failure and betrayal and loneliness I felt at New Life Church. I don't want to go back to these places.

But I have to. If I don't, I'll come up with self-destructive ways of dealing with the pain. As Allender says, I have to enter that story. Because it's *my* story. It shapes who I am even to this day. All the shame, all the failure, all the embarrassment and insecurity I felt as a kid, a teenager, a young adult, a pastor, a husband, a father, a friend, a sinner. I have to listen to that story again and again, lest I disintegrate and hide just like I used to. To be a pastor of broken people requires that I come out of hiding and share my brokenness with them. Otherwise I'll use them to get the affirmation I'm longing for. I'll use God to get people to like me. And

---

4. "The Day I Gave My Heart Away," by Billy Crockett/Kenny Wood. ©1989 Word Music, LLC. All Rights Reserved. Used by Permission.

I'll become someone like King Saul: envious, hypocritical, self-centered, idolatrous, mean, alone. Ironically, it brings healing to the body of Christ when I share my story. Brennan Manning says, "In a futile attempt to erase our past, we deprive the community of our healing gift. If we conceal our wounds out of fear and shame, our inner darkness can neither be illuminated nor become a light for others ... [G]race and healing are communicated through the vulnerability of men and women who have been fractured and heartbroken by life."[5]

My story also helps me understand some of the struggles I've had and mistakes I've made as a pastor. Why do I exhaust myself and exasperate my family by saying yes to an unending list of tasks, meetings, appointments, and requests? It's because if I say no, someone may not like me. Why do I often leave elder meetings feeling like a failure? It's because in the faces of my elders I often see the glare of a father who could never be pleased. Why did I uproot my family from a church where we were happy and making a difference, and move hundreds of miles away to a large church filled with problems? Was it really because I sensed the call of God? Or could it have also been because the prestige of New Life Church represented the A+ on my report card, the approval of my parents, the slap on the back saying, "Welcome to the inner circle"? Honestly, I think it was a little bit of both.

After thirty years of pastoral ministry I am still discovering the many ways my story operates both as curse and blessing. Dan Allender writes, "If stories are one of the primary ways we achieve self-understanding and one of the central means by which leaders create meaning for their organizations, then it is imperative to listen well to the stories that give us a sense of who we are."[6]

Knowing your story will not prevent church hurricanes. You will still make mistakes and be sinned against. Problems will still disrupt the progress of the gospel in your church and city. But knowing your story will make it much less likely that you will be the reason for the storm. Only the pastor with a healthy amount

---

5. Manning, *Abba's Child*, 29.
6. Allender, *Leading with a Limp*, 47.

Part 1: Crisis Readiness

of self-knowledge can recognize when she is using the ministry for personal glorification, and repent. Only the pastor who understands his story can say no when asked to do something unethical or unwise, and do the right thing. Only that pastor has the courage to refuse to bow down before the Golden Calf. Only that pastor can be honest about her sins and weaknesses, ask for help, admit need, or turn down a job opportunity for which she's not qualified or gifted. Self-knowledge liberates you from a Messiah complex. It frees you to do what you love and delegate everything else. It releases you from the pressure to make people happy and solve every problem. In short, it makes ministry much more fun.

Peter Scazzero, in his book *The Emotionally Healthy Church*, says, "Discipleship . . . must include honest reflection on the positive and negative impact of my family of origin as well as other major influences in my life. This is hard work. But the extent to which we can go back and understand how it has shaped us will determine, to a large degree, our level of awareness and our ability to break destructive patterns, pass on constructive legacies, and grow in love toward God and people."[7]

John Calvin would agree. The better I know my story, in all its "shaming nakedness" (per Calvin), the better I know God and the faster I run to Jesus, who, "because he himself has suffered when tempted . . . is able to help those who are being tempted" (Heb 2:18).

In fact, that's what I did one afternoon in the spring of 1975. I ran to Jesus. I'd had it up to here with the good-little-boy routine. I knew it was fake. It wasn't the real me. So, like Eustace in C. S. Lewis's *The Voyage of the Dawn Treader*, I let Aslan "un-dragon" me. I took out a legal pad and wrote down all the sins and problems I knew I had in my life. I admitted all the lies, all the hiding, all the fears of which I was aware. I confessed my guilt and shame and asked Jesus to forgive me and take me into his family. One layer of sin after another had to go. As Eustace put it, "[I]t hurt

---

7. Scazzero and Bird, *Emotionally Healthy Church*, 99.

Know Yourself

worse than anything I've ever felt. The only thing that made me able to bear it was just the pleasure of feeling the stuff peel off. You know—if you've ever picked the scab off a sore place. It hurts like billy-oh but it is such fun to see it coming away."[8]

Now, forty-plus years later, I find that I need Jesus to un-dragon me every single day.

The last verse of Billy Crockett's song speaks eloquently of my experience of God's grace, and I trust yours too:

> One night he sat up in the dark 'cause he couldn't sleep
> And wondered if he'd die alone with nothing fit to keep
> Into his darkest darkness there without a soul to see,
> Someone came and something changed, the I became a We
> The little boy was not alone, the grown-up shed his skin
> The frightened heart was not so scared because Someone came in
> He took my heart for his own home, and let me know I'm not alone
> My life was changed I'm glad to say the day I gave my heart away.[9]

It bears repeating: You minister out of who you are.

---

8. Lewis, *Voyage of the Dawn Treader*, 474–475.

9. "The Day I Gave My Heart Away," by Billy Crockett/Kenny Wood. ©1989 Word Music, LLC. All Rights Reserved. Used by Permission.

Chapter 5

Build Up the Levees

When Hurricane Katrina hit the Gulf Coast on Monday, August 29, 2005, it became obvious that the levees of New Orleans, built decades earlier, had not been designed for a hurricane of that intensity. In a press conference on August 28 Mayor Nagin predicted, "The storm surge most likely will topple our levee system."[1] And topple it did. Katrina caused record storm surges all up and down the coast—in some places as high as thirty-four feet. New Orleans was especially unfortunate. The Big Easy sits six feet below sea level. Do the math; her levees were useless. By the evening of August 30, eighty percent of the city was submerged under water. Fifty-three breaches of the levee system occurred in greater New Orleans, leading to catastrophic flooding and loss of life, limb, and property. Not until October 11 were all the floodwaters gone.

My paternal grandfather was a civil engineer who worked on the New Orleans levees in the 1920s, so I know something about them. We get our word *levee* from the French verb *lever*, meaning to raise. We use a thing called a *lever* to lift something heavy. We take an *elevator* to go up. When we raise something higher we say that we *elevate* it. You get the idea. A *levee* is an earthen structure or a wall of sandbags raised up alongside a body of water to prevent flooding.

---

1. Nagin and Blanco, Press Conference, Aug. 28, 2005.

Build Up the Levees

So what must be raised up in order to protect a congregation or a church staff from the floodwaters of sin and dissension? *Trust.* Trust is the levee system of a church. When the trust level is high, storms will come, but their damage will be contained. And if I've learned anything from my years in ministry it is that you cannot work too soon, too hard, or too long to earn the trust of the people you lead.

When I arrived as the pastor of New Life, I knew I needed to invest a significant amount of time and energy building up the levees of trust in the church. My two predecessors had abused the congregation. One had bossed people around, using his power to push the church in the direction he thought it should take. The other had an adulterous affair with a church member, using his charisma to charm her and deceive everyone else. Needless to say, the members of New Life Church did not have a very good impression of pastors. Staff members and church officers were on guard and didn't want to be hurt again.

I needed to exhibit a different model of pastoral leadership.

I read Ezekiel 34 over and over, praying that God's indictment of the shepherds of Israel would never apply to me. In that chapter God says to pastors,

> . . . should not shepherds feed the sheep? You eat the fat, you clothe yourselves with the wool, you slaughter the fat ones, but you do not feed the sheep. The weak you have not strengthened, the sick you have not healed, the injured you have not bound up, the strayed you have not brought back, the lost you have not sought, and with force and harshness you have ruled them. So they were scattered, because there was no shepherd . . . (Ezek 34:2–5)

God goes on to reassure his people through Ezekiel that he will do what the selfish shepherds of Israel had failed to do: "I myself will be the shepherd of my sheep, and I myself will make them lie down, declares the Lord God" (Ezek 34:15). Of course, this is an Old Testament prophecy looking forward to Jesus Christ, the

Good Shepherd who knows his sheep and lays down his life for them (John 10:14–15).

Like the people of Israel in Ezekiel's day, the sheep of New Life Church were hurting. They desperately needed their new shepherd to listen to them, to grieve with them, to know and be known by them. Another senior pastor leading "with force and harshness" would have been a disaster. There would be time later to draft a vision statement, introduce new programs, do an outreach and promote a stewardship campaign. But now was not that time. What the people needed most in those first months of my pastorate was a long period of calm led by a pastor willing to love them and earn their trust.

So before I moved onto the field in August, I contacted the church secretary and asked her to arrange a series of small group gatherings in homes for my first few months at New Life. We called them "Welcome Mat Desserts." I wanted everyone in the church to be invited. So the secretary split up the membership roster geographically, recruited hosts, and sent out hundreds of invitations. To make it doable for the hosts and easy for me to get to know people, I wanted no more than a dozen attendees at each gathering. The church had over 500 members, so even if just half the people accepted my invitation it would take one or two desserts a week to get around to everyone by Thanksgiving. But I knew it would be worth the time and effort. As soon as my wife and I moved into our home we started attending these gatherings. Several months (and pounds) later, we had met personally about two-thirds of the congregation in various homes. At each dessert my wife and I shared our story. More importantly, we listened to their stories—their disappointments and fears, their hopes and dreams for the church. It was one of the best things I could have done to begin shoring up the levees of trust in the church.

I also knew I needed to be strategic with my choice of sermons in those early days. If there was one thing the people needed to hear week after week it was the gospel—the good news of God's amazing love and grace. So for my first sermon series I chose an exposition of Galatians. A congregation submerged in law and hurt by sin desperately needed the freeing power of grace.

In addition, it was essential that I build a relationship with my fellow staff members. On my team were an associate pastor, youth pastor, worship pastor, missions director, preschool director, three secretaries, and bookstore manager. My wife and I hosted most of these people in our home and I scheduled several hours a week with them. I socialized with the other pastors outside our normal ministry routine. We shared meals and had fun together. I led weekly staff meetings and expected everyone to be there. In those meetings we spent time praying for each other as well as doing the business of the church.

I wanted New Life to know that I could be trusted, and building trust takes time—especially in a hurting church. I've always been fascinated by Jesus' leisurely pace. If there was ever a man on a mission, it was the Lord Jesus Christ. But reading through the four gospels gives the impression that Jesus was never hurried. He had lots to do but was not "busy," in the modern, frazzled sense of the word. Instead, he focused on relationships with people—around food and drink, at parties, strolling along the road, sitting with moms and their children, gazing out at the sea with fishermen. I wanted to model that unhurried, person-to-person kind of ministry at New Life. It soon became apparent, however, that staff members were not used to my slow, relational style. I had only been in the office a couple days when one of the secretaries expressed frustration to an elder that I was not already issuing orders to the staff. I said, "I'm not ready to give orders. Be patient. I need to learn my way around, get to know people, and figure out priorities. For now, just keep doing what you've been doing." At this stage in my pastorate, establishing trust was Priority One. Pastor Joon Tavarez of Brandon, Florida, says, "Trust is rarely the result of one specific event. It is usually something that develops from a significant amount of time in relationship—sort of like aged wine: the older the relationship, the better."[2]

---

2. Tavarez, "Wine Gets Better with Jesus, Not Age," lines 4–6.

Part 1: Crisis Readiness

What is trust? Author Robert Porter Lynch defines trust as the absence of fear in a relationship. Positively, trust is a reliance that "you will be there for me when I need you; you won't sacrifice me for your self interest; [and] you can be counted on to work for my best interests as well as yours."[3]

Of course, to build trust one must first be trustworthy. Trustworthiness is an essential character trait for those who lead. Jethro's advice to his overworked son-in-law Moses was to "look for able men from all the people, men who fear God, who are trustworthy and hate a bribe, and place such men over the people as chiefs of thousands, of hundreds, of fifties, and of tens. And let them judge the people at all times" (Exod 18:21–22). The psalmist can call us to "Trust in [God] at all times" because God is trustworthy; he is "a refuge for us" (Ps 62:8). God's words are "trustworthy and true" (Rev 21:5).

How can you earn the trust of those you lead? Here are ten ways:

1. Communicate with clarity. Say what you mean, and mean what you say.
2. Have the hard conversations. Tell people your expectations and let them know when they fail to meet them.
3. Be the first and best repenter. Admit your mistakes. Ask for forgiveness from those affected by them. Even if you think you *may* have sinned against someone, take the initiative to talk to that person (Matt 5:23–24).
4. Open yourself to critique and feedback. Ask people, "How are you experiencing me? What can I do to improve our working relationship?"
5. Obey the rules you set for others. If you expect your team to be on time for a meeting, be on time yourself.

---

3. Lynch, "Building the Pillar of Trust," 1.

BUILD UP THE LEVEES

6. Keep the promises you make. (Remember George H. W. Bush's famous words, "Read my lips . . .."?)
7. Be consistent. Don't keep moving the game plan or the goalposts. Be the same person no matter whom you are with.
8. Run a transparent organization. Share information. Don't try to protect people from the truth. It's the truth that sets us free.
9. Carefully choose your allies. If you align yourself with the wrong people, you may compromise your integrity.
10. Ask for help. Collaborate. Don't act like you can do things better yourself, because you can't.

Do not dare minimize the importance of these ten things. Someone has said, "Trust is hard to earn, easy to lose, and tremendously hard to rebuild." Leaders can be, and often are, abusive, controlling, narcissistic individuals. Everyone knows a leader who has blown it.

Everyone has known the disappointment of following someone only to find out they were heading for a cliff. As Dan Allender says, ". . . a leader will at some point misuse the power of his position."[4] This is why the words of Pastor Scott Sauls should be heeded: "[T]rust, and especially the vulnerability that comes with trust, must be earned . . . It took a direct word from God for Ananias to move past his appropriate caution concerning Paul. It also took fourteen years for Paul, who was formerly Saul of Tarsus, to learn the ways of grace and gain the trust of the Christian community, before he would begin his missionary journeys and letter-writing to the churches . . ."[5]

There are no shortcuts to earning the trust of those you have been called to serve.

The early trust earning steps I took at New Life Church appeared to point us in a positive direction. However, as time went on I

---

4. Allender, *Leading with a Limp*, 61.
5. Sauls, "Sometimes, I Would Almost Rather Be Damned," lines 94–105.

made two mistakes that caused a breach in the levees. One was that I introduced changes to the Sunday morning worship service too soon. In chapter 1 I described some of these changes. I assumed people would welcome contemporary worship songs led by guitars and drums. Some did; many did not. I should have made sure that I had the full support of the elder board before changing the order and feel of a worship service that had taken twenty years to establish. A good rule of thumb is to not make any big changes during your first year of ministry in a church. And at New Life, a change in the worship service was a really big change—bigger than I recognized.

The other mistake I made at New Life was being too accommodating to strong personalities in the church. New Life Church, like every church, was comprised of two groups of people. One group was happy and agreeable; they were there to enjoy the ride. The other group was the malcontents. They weren't happy unless they were driving the train. Several individuals in the latter group I found particularly intimidating. One day, two power brokers took me out to lunch and urged me to do something to rattle the dry bones. "Pastor, this church is going to go nowhere unless you shake things up. Do something dramatic. Pull out all the stops." While it may have been true that New Life needed new life, their message was, "C'mon, you need to be stronger. Make a stand. Use your bully pulpit to get people riled up. If members leave, so be it. That may be just what needs to happen."

I should have said, "Thank you for your input. I'll think about it and get back to you." But I didn't.

By this time in my ministry at New Life I'd been tossed this way and that by crisis after crisis. I was tired, frustrated, and discouraged. Unwisely, I agreed to do what these men recommended. The next Sunday would be a day no one would soon forget; I would lay it on the line. When Sunday morning arrived, I went into the green room and told the choir they would not be needed that day. They were shocked but they dutifully hung up their choir robes and took a seat in the congregation. We started the worship service with a single hymn and a short prayer. Then I launched into my sermon. For a solid hour I took people to the woodshed. My text was Luke 10:25-37, the story of the Good Samaritan. I chastised members of the church who, like the priest and the Levite who passed by the injured man on the road, had been ignoring the needs of our community. I called New Life to a radical commitment to get out of our comfort zones and welcome the stranger, the poor, and the unlovable into our church family. While that's a perfectly biblical thing to call Christians to, my delivery was graceless and condemning. I also threw a few barbs at people who had criticized the worship changes I'd made. It was not a gospel-centered, hope-giving sermon. And it had two effects: While one group of members was puffed up and happy that I'd thrown down the gauntlet, another group felt put down, condemned, and ostracized. Not a few of them left the church and never came back.

It was a sinful, insensitive move on my part. It's one thing to call God's people to mission and obedience but quite another to do so in a harsh way. Remember God's words to the shepherds of Israel in Ezekiel 34? With "force and harshness" they had ruled the sheep (Ezek 34:4). By contrast, of Jesus it was said that "a bruised reed he will not break, and a smoldering wick he will not quench" (Matt 12:20). His yoke is easy, his burden is light (Matt 11:30). I did a lot of breaking and quenching that Sunday, and many people went home feeling burdened rather than lifted up.

What did I do wrong? I let the voices of strong people pressure me into violating my own philosophy of ministry. This is not an uncommon error for pastors; by nature most of us are people-pleasers. Thom Rainer, who pastored four churches before becoming the president and CEO of LifeWay Christian Resources, admits to "nine stupid things" he did as a pastor, one of which was yielding to unreasonable demands and requests.[6] By accommodating the wishes of powerful men eager for a fight, I needlessly offended a portion of my congregation and lost their trust. Later, I publicly apologized for my angry sermon. But by that time the floodwaters

---

6. Rainer, "Nine Stupid Things I Did as a Pastor," lines 34-36.

of dissension had overtopped the levees. I had lost my capital. A year after preaching that sermon, I was gone.

Author J. R. Briggs writes, ". . . one of the frightening things about the wilderness is how many voices you hear in it. It is hard to discern between the voices—which ones are truthful and worthy of our attention and which are dangerous and should be ignored."[7] Be very careful to whom you listen. The wrong voices will cause potentially irreparable harm to you and your ministry.

Do you want to prepare your church for the storms that will surely come? The most important thing you can do is to start earning trust as soon as your pastorate begins. And this never stops. Your staff must trust that you are honest and reliable. Your volunteers must trust that you do not wish merely to use them but value their partnership. Your members must trust that you are true to your word and have their best interests at heart. The trust you win now will be there to protect you when the hurricane hits.

---

7. Briggs, *Fail*, 113.

Chapter 6
Focus!

My mantra in this book has been that storms, skirmishes, and struggles are inevitable in pastoral ministry. It's supposed to be that way because of our sinful human nature, the opposition of Satan, and the inherent difficulty of caring for the souls of diverse and broken people. But it is possible to diminish and even avoid certain problems, if you, your leadership team, and your congregation have a clear vision of the future and stay focused on that vision.

There is no shortage of books and articles about vision. A complete treatment of the subject is beyond the scope of this book. For the purpose of this chapter, let me offer a truism: *All the great leaders and organizations throughout history have been about one big thing.* What was the thirteenth-century Scot, William Wallace, passionate about? Freedom. Martin Luther King, Jr.? Equal rights for African Americans. Mother Teresa? Remedying the plight of the poor. The Wright Brothers? Human flight. Steve Jobs? A simpler computer. What has made McDonald's the world's largest hamburger chain? Hamburgers (not artisan chicken sandwiches and frappés). Did Colonel Sanders get rich saying that sushi is "finger-lickin' good"? Did Martina Navratilova play checkers? Did Tom Clancy try to write romance novels? Did Vince Lombardi become a dance instructor? No, no, no! It was by focusing on one thing, and doing it relentlessly, that these people and organizations changed the world.

Jim Collins, whose book *Good to Great* has sold millions of copies and been translated into over thirty languages, talks about the ancient Greek parable of the fox and the hedgehog.[1] According to this parable, a fox knows many small things, while a hedgehog knows one big thing. Hedgehogs view the world through the lens of a single, defining idea, while foxes look at the world in piecemeal fashion. Professor Alison Gopnik offers this analysis: "Hedgehogs have a single grand idea that they apply to everything, while foxes come up with a new idea for every situation."[2]

Perhaps this oversimplifies the universe of leaders, but when it comes to the work of a pastor it is the hedgehog approach that builds a strong, stable environment for discipleship. As our world grows increasingly complex and confounding, people need a "single grand idea," a simple, clear picture of a better future. That picture is vision. Without it, according to various translations of Proverbs 29:18, "the people perish" (KJV) or "cast off restraint" (ESV) or "run wild" (HCSB). Father Theodore Hesburgh, who was president of the University of Notre Dame for thirty-five years, once said, "The very essence of leadership is that you have to have vision. It's got to be a vision you articulate clearly and forcefully on every occasion. You can't blow an uncertain trumpet."[3]

Discord thrives in the Petri dish of inconsistency. While, of course, you must be sensitive to the leading of the Spirit and the changing times in which we live, constantly altering your priorities will dampen the enthusiasm of your congregation and damage your credibility. I remember a congregational meeting in which plans for the coming year were announced. I overheard a church member whisper to another, "Don't get too excited. Next year everything will change." No wonder that church had a hard time recruiting volunteers.

1. Collins, *Good to Great*, 90–119.
2. Gopnik, "In Life, Who Wins, the Fox or the Hedgehog?" lines 5–6.
3. Totman, *Ironies Leaders Navigate*, 47.

Focus!

I pastored a church in rural South Carolina for seven years. We came up with a simple phrase to articulate our vision: "Making Disciples for Christ." We had spent considerable time looking at biblical principles, my gifts and passions, the needs of our community, and the makeup of our congregation. The elders and I spent many hours in prayer, conversation, and Bible study. We also got members of the congregation involved in brainstorming sessions and prayer. The result was a strong vision for making disciples. We defined a disciple as a growing, committed follower of Jesus. We determined that in order to make disciples we needed to do one thing really well: teach the Word of God. We did not do small groups. We did not try to build a big choir or music ministry. We did not offer our community a preschool or a sports ministry. There's nothing wrong with these things, and in other churches I've pastored we have tackled those programs and more. But in this church we decided early on that we were going to focus on teaching and preaching the Bible to the best of our ability. So I spent a lot of my time preparing sermons and Sunday school lessons. When hiring a youth pastor and an associate pastor we looked for people who were theologically sharp and able to teach. We used a Vacation Bible School curriculum that included tons of Bible memorization. We turned our Sunday evening worship service into a teaching time. We built an educational wing so we could offer more Sunday school classes. Vision guided our planning.

In the church I currently serve, we summed up our vision with the phrase "The Cross-Shaped Life." We dream of a church characterized by four things, as shown on the cross below:

Part 1: Crisis Readiness

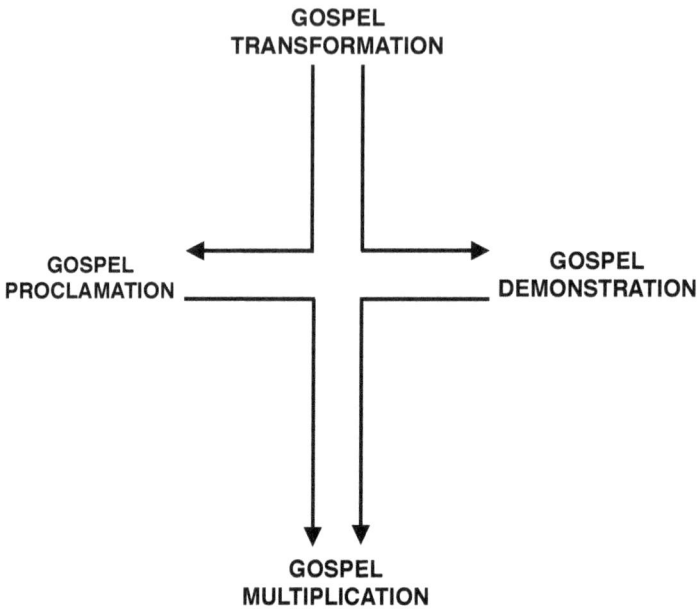

To add clarity, we wrote ends statements for the four dimensions of The Cross-Shaped Life:

- *Gospel Transformation (discipleship):* Disciples become Christlike in moral character and missional conduct.

- *Gospel Proclamation (evangelism):* Disciples meet the spiritual needs of people in our city and other strategic world locations.

- *Gospel Demonstration (mercy/justice):* Disciples meet the physical needs of people in our city and other strategic world locations.

- *Gospel Multiplication (church planting):* Disciples increase the number of disciples, Life Groups, and congregations in our city and other strategic world locations.

Your church's vision should be different from the above examples. Never borrow another church's vision statement just because you like it. Your church has a unique set of gifts and talents and a unique role in your community. You can't do everything. So what is the *one big thing* your church will be about? It can be an exciting, galvanizing process to discover God's vision for your congregation and pursue it relentlessly.

It's easy to get hung up on semantics. Words like vision, mission, strategy, goals, tactics . . . they can get awfully confusing. What's the difference between "mission" and "vision"? You may have your own definitions, but I see those terms like this:

- *Mission* is God's big purpose for his church as spelled out in the Great Commission, "Go therefore and make disciples of all nations, baptizing them in the name of the Father and of the Son and of the Holy Spirit, teaching them to observe all that I have commanded you" (Matt 28:19–20). By this definition, every church has the same mission: to make disciples of Jesus Christ.

- *Vision* is your church's dream of what making disciples looks like in your context. It should be captured by a one-sentence, inspiring statement that describes the desired change resulting from your church's ministry. By this definition, every church could have a vision that is different from every other church.

To illustrate, here are the vision statements of several large churches in America:[4]

- The Journey (St. Louis): "Growing disciples, starting churches"
- The Rock (San Diego): "To be a global and highly trusted model of relevant and innovative evangelism"
- NewSpring Church (Anderson, SC): "To continue growing, impacting lives and using technology and the arts to reach 100,000 people for Jesus Christ"

---

4. Van Korlaar, "30+ Examples of Church Vision Statements," lines 26–152.

Part 1: Crisis Readiness

- Coral Ridge Presbyterian Church (Ft. Lauderdale): "To rescue and replenish a world lost and broken by sin, thereby 'making all things new'"
- Missio Dei Church (Cincinnati): "To see the people of Cincinnati forever changed by the gospel of Jesus and holding dear to him as their source of all joy and worth"

Vision statements like these have a marvelous effect upon the people of God. They do not just increase awareness about the church. They paint a mental picture of a preferable future, thereby motivating people to contribute their time, talents, and treasure. The fact is, people long to dream. They need to look up from the trivial stuff of earth and gaze heavenward. This is why people do social media, join clubs, donate to charities, attend political rallies, sign petitions, start companies, and go to football games. Vision fills the need of the human heart to participate in something that transcends self. The French writer and poet, Antoine de Saint-Exupéry, is said to have said, "If you want to build a ship, don't herd people together to collect wood and don't assign them tasks and work, but rather teach them to long for the endless immensity of the sea." A church with vision is a church filled with volunteers and stakeholders.

Vision statements also help keep a church from getting distracted. There are countless good things for which a church might spend its time and resources. But the good is the enemy of the best. A "hedgehog church" focused on one big idea is likely to be more unified, excited, and impactful than a "fox church" scurrying around trying to do everything that might be done. Therefore, as you develop your church's vision you will discover the need to gently but resolutely say no. A church member once came to me asking me to get involved with his prison ministry. "Your prison ministry is a great thing," I explained. "But it's not part of our church's vision right now. I love what you're doing, and I'll pray for you, but I can't add it to my plate or promote it from up front."

Of course, when you say no to a program or activity, you are sure to upset someone—or a group of someones. Dan Allender writes, "The paradox of death leading to life requires that you disappoint many to please One. It requires you to say no much more than you say yes."[5] My friend with the prison ministry ended up leaving our church and going elsewhere. That hurt. Canceling a church ministry that has been in place for years is like sticking a needle into a child's palm to remove a splinter. It will not be done without pain. But in the long run, removing the splinter frees a child from the bigger problem of infection. Similarly, keeping a church program going simply because "it's what we've always done" is hurting the church in unseen ways. Every yes to one good program is a no to something better. Push through the pain of saying no and you will have a church more focused on God's calling. The more focused you are, the greater the likelihood of weathering the storms of ministry.

How can you and your team develop a vision that honors God and prepares your church for the future? Here are ten steps that have proven effective in other churches:

1. Decide that you will not be in a hurry. Take your time. Developing your church's vision could easily take six to twelve months or more.

2. Pull your leaders together and spend a significant amount of time praying for God's vision for your church to become your vision. Pray throughout the process.

3. Let the congregation know you are seeking God's vision for your church. Ask them to pray. Invite them to attend meetings of the leadership and offer their input.

4. Study the four gospels, the book of Acts, Paul's letter to the Ephesians, 1 Timothy, and other key passages of the Bible. Look for vision principles from the ministry of Jesus and the early church.

5. Identify the main needs of your community. Get a demographic study and draw conclusions about the makeup of your community. What are its strengths and weaknesses,

---

5. Allender, *Leading with a Limp*, 136.

Part 1: Crisis Readiness

its prevailing sins and persistent problems? What are other churches doing to impact your community? How might your church partner with them?

6. Study your congregation. What are your church's strengths and weaknesses? What can your church do as well or better than any other church? What is your church poor at doing? What should your church stop doing? What has your church been most passionate about over time? Where has the movement of God's Spirit been most evident in the church's history?

7. After a sufficient amount of time has been given to this process, draft a vision statement and present it to your leadership for their consideration. Sit with it for a while. Make needed revisions.

8. Present the vision statement to the church at a congregational meeting. Invite feedback. Pray over the statement for several weeks as a church. Listen to the people's questions and suggestions.

9. As a leadership team, formally adopt the finished vision statement.

10. Present the statement to the church family. Use it to launch a sermon series on the vision of the church. Display the statement everywhere you can. Refer to it often. Use it as a basis for decision making and programming. Pray about it in the Sunday morning intercessory prayer.

Ministry storms are an inevitable part of a faithful pastor's experience. Taking steps such as those outlined in this section will help prevent more of them from happening and reduce their destructive impact.

> **Summary of Part 1: Crisis Readiness**
>
> - Expect the hurricane. Don't be taken by surprise.
> - Become as familiar as possible with your church's unique history and culture.
> - Know who you are. Study and share your own story.
> - Earn and preserve the trust of your congregation.
> - Lead your church in developing a simple vision for the future, and stay focused on it.

Part 2

Crisis Response

Chapter 7
Teamwork

IN PART 1 WE looked at how to prepare yourself and your church for the inevitable church hurricane. Despite your best efforts at averting or minimizing the damage, churches of every size experience ministry-threatening storms. In Part 2 we will explore six responses a pastor must make when the winds are howling in order to lead his church through conflict into sunnier weather.

To introduce this chapter, I have to tell you about my grandson Augustine. At age three, Auggie had this habit of going around his house and gathering up as many items in his arms as he possibly could—an early form of multitasking, I suppose. We have this photo of Auggie that still cracks me up. Dressed in Teenage Mutant Ninja Turtles pajamas, he's holding a Star Wars light saber in his left hand and clutching a stuffed Disney bear under his left arm. He's got his plaid security blanket over his right shoulder, a pacifier in his mouth, and a Lone Ranger mask over his eyes. The perfectly serious look on his face says, "Don't mess with me. I can handle anything."

That photo, comical though it be, makes me think of how we pastors often feel. Take today, for example. My schedule says I'm a counselor, preacher, writer, small groups pastor, discipler of men, wedding officiant, administrator, organizational leader, financial consultant, teacher, and event planner. Not to mention my obligatory roles as a mystic, philosopher, Bible scholar, prayer warrior, chaplain, mind-reader, peacemaker, problem solver, social media expert, political commentator, pop culture critic, entertainer, fundraiser, fitness magazine cover model, and community activist. Oh, and somewhere in there I'm a husband, father, and grandfather.

It's impossible.

Yet we labor on, picking up duty after duty, attending event after event, saying yes to request after request, wearing our best pastoral smile and our Lone Ranger mask. We've worn that mask so long we even think like the Lone Ranger: "Don't mess with me; I can handle anything. I have gifts, experience, and Jesus. What more do I need? Bring it on."

That ministry philosophy will not get you or your congregation through a monster church hurricane.

What lies beneath the Lone Ranger mentality? In many ministers of the gospel (and in my own heart) there is a prideful inflation of our own abilities and resistance to receiving help from others. Instead of the Mary Kay motto, "You can have it all," we've adopted the motto, "You can *do* it all." We want to be superheroes who rescue our poor parishioners in distress—and, incidentally, receive their adulation. We want people to think we're omnipotent, omniscient, and omnipresent. It's our way of building a record and earning righteousness apart from Christ. Depending on other people indicates weakness. And weakness, say Michigan psychologists Dane Ver Merris and Bert van Hoek, is what many pastors are loath to reveal:

> Ministers are understandably reluctant to admit shortcomings on the psychological tests we use. Instead, pastors view themselves as highly principled, moral, and virtuous. Test instruments are quite good at detecting this defensiveness, and the pastors we have counseled often have been reluctant to admit even minor flaws or emotional discomfort—even to the point of threatening the validity of the test results. Rather than be surprised (or unduly troubled) by pastors' strong tendency to be defensive, those who are in a position to help must simply acknowledge the strong pressure pastors feel to make

Teamwork

a polished presentation of themselves in spite of their obvious and genuine struggles.[1]

Ver Merris and van Hoek's observations come from years of working with burned out pastors. They go on to say that emotionally healthy pastors "accept criticism with grace, have a realistic notion of their own worth, [and] value positive interpersonal relationships . . ." In other words, resisting the Lone Ranger mentality is key to effective pastoral ministry.

Our church recently started a coed cycling club. Every Saturday morning, we meet in the church parking lot, hop on our road bikes, and go for a ride of thirty miles or more. It's turning out to be a good outreach, as several nonchurchgoers have joined our little band. I'm learning how important it is to stay in the paceline and cycle as close as possible to the bike in front of me. This is called drafting. Each cyclist creates a vortex, or a low pressure area, that pulls the next cyclist forward. It is far easier to be behind someone and benefit from their draft than to be alone or out in front. "Cyclists who are part of the group can save up to forty percent in energy expenditures over a cyclist who is not drafting with the group," says scientist Paul Doherty.[2]

In like fashion, your ministry will be easier—and a lot more fun—when you rely on the help of other people.

Are you a Lone Ranger pastor? Here's a simple way to find out. Circle yes or no to the following questions:

1. Do you feel you are the only one in the church who can do most things well?

    Yes   No

2. Do you easily take offense when someone critiques your sermons?

    Yes   No

---

1. Ver Merris and Van Hoek, "How Pastors Struggle," lines 14–22.
2. Doherty, "Science of Cycling: Aerodynamics & Drafting," lines 35–39.

PART 2: CRISIS RESPONSE

3. Are your sermon illustrations more about your successes than your failures?

    Yes   No

4. Do you resist delegating tasks?

    Yes   No

5. Do you feel the need to have the last word on discussions around the church?

    Yes   No

6. Is it difficult for you to admit when you are wrong?

    Yes   No

7. Are you too busy?

    Yes   No

8. Do you have a hard time letting a guest speaker or another pastor preach on Sundays?

    Yes   No

9. Are you lonely?

    Yes   No

10. Do you feel the need to be in charge of every group or event you attend?

    Yes   No

If you answered yes to many of those questions, you need to wake up to what you are doing to both yourself and those you lead. Pastors are not called by God to be Lone Rangers. Even if you say, "Jesus and I can handle it," Jesus did not come to be your Tonto. Despite what the bumper sticker says, he's not your co-pilot. Yes, he is with us to the very end of the age, but Jesus is far more than our heavenly assistant. He is King and Head of the church. He died on the cross, rose again, and ascended to heaven in order to make us members of "a chosen race, a royal priesthood, a holy nation, a people for his own possession, that [we] may proclaim the excellencies of him who called [us] out of darkness into his marvelous light" (1 Pet 2:9). We are not isolated individuals who believe in Jesus, but "living stones" interconnected with other believers (1 Pet 2:5). These stones are "being joined together . . . into a dwelling place for God by the Spirit" (Eph 2:21–22). Every stone is important. Every soldier is needed for the battle. The Holy Spirit has strategically placed people in our churches with the gifts required to accomplish his will. To deprive our members of opportunities to use those gifts is to sin against them and hinder God's work. The job of a pastor is "to equip the saints for the work of ministry, for building up the body of Christ" until "each part is working properly" (Eph 4:12–16).

When I was starting out as a pastor, I set a high bar for myself. I tried to visit hospitalized parishioners every day, even those who were getting simple outpatient procedures. I tried to call every single church member on his or her birthday. I tried writing thank-you notes to every volunteer several times a year. I tried to call every widow on the anniversary of her husband's death. I tried to visit every family in the church on an annual basis. I tried to lead worship Sunday morning, Sunday evening, and Wednesday evening. I tried to teach every new member's class. I tried to lead a home group Bible study every week. Notice the key words: "I tried, tried, tried." I was running myself ragged until a friend asked me why I felt compelled to do all those things. Did I think I was the only person in the church capable of doing them? Thanks to that bold friend, I realized I was breaking the eighth commandment. I was stealing ministry opportunities from the people of God. What is worse, I was breaking the first and second commandments. I was putting my ministry abilities ahead of God's and worshiping the idol of human approval. Since those early days I have learned that repentance means not trying to be Jesus for my church. Like John the Baptist in John 1:20, I've learned to remind myself and tell others, "I am not the Messiah." Visiting people in the hospital is a good thing; but not when it encourages people to put more trust in me than in Jesus. Phone calls and thank-you notes are good things; but not when I use them merely to ingratiate myself to my church members. Leading worship and teaching classes and Bible studies are good things; but not when it denies that opportunity to other gifted leaders in the church.

Author Kevin DeYoung in his book *Crazy Busy* points out that even Jesus didn't do it all:

> Jesus didn't meet every need. He left people waiting in line to be healed. He left one town to preach to another. He hid away to pray. He got tired. He never interacted with the vast majority of people on the planet. He spent thirty years in training and only three years in ministry. He did not try to do it all. And yet, he did everything God asked him to do.[3]

How unexpected: the second Person of the Trinity—God incarnate—relied on the help of twelve men, one of whom was a fake, to get world evangelization off and running. He could have easily done it all. But he used teamwork instead.

The point I am making here is that when storms of deception, discord, discontent, or dissension hit your church, Jesus is not all you need. "Jesus and I can handle it" sounds spiritual enough, but it's a thin disguise for isolation and self-promotion. If the Bible's teaching on the church means anything, it means you need a team of people to walk through the storm with you. You need their advice, prayers, rebukes, and tears. You need them to preach the gospel to you. You need them to be your ally with difficult people. You need them to help you brainstorm a way out of the mess. You need them to speak truth, to yourself and to others.

Does this sound like heresy—"Jesus is not all you need"? Of course it's heresy if we're talking about salvation. We are saved by grace alone through faith alone in Christ alone. But in the everyday world of battling sin, making disciples, shepherding the church, and spreading the gospel, we need more than Jesus.

In Genesis 2, Adam found out Jesus is not all we need. Adam had not yet fallen into sin. A beautiful world filled with friendly animals and gorgeous vegetation lay at his feet. He had purposeful,

---

3. DeYoung, *Crazy Busy*, Kindle Edition: Chapter 4.

enjoyable work to do. Best of all, he had unbroken fellowship with God. But God said, "It is not good that the man should be alone" (Gen 2:18). Adam needed people. Particularly a person with a figure.

In Exodus 17, Moses discovered Jesus is not all we need. The people of Israel had left Egypt and were on their way to the Promised Land when they were attacked by fierce Amalekites. While Joshua led the fighting down below in Rephidim, Moses interceded for the soldiers from his perch on a hill. The text says, "Whenever Moses held up his hand, Israel prevailed, and whenever he lowered his hand, Amalek prevailed" (Exod 17:11). Before long Moses grew tired of holding up his hands. So he called for Aaron and Hur, who held up his arms while he prayed for victory below. The Israelites prevailed because Moses didn't try to go it alone. He needed people.

Who is your Aaron? Who is your Hur? It's not good for you to be alone.

I am a Presbyterian pastor. That means I function as one of the elders of my church. I am called a teaching elder, and they are ruling elders. Together we lead our church. I have no greater authority than they. I am accountable to them. So in Presbyterian polity, there is a built-in antidote to the Lone Ranger mentality. Your church may operate differently. But surely there are people in your congregation whom you can recruit to be your "crisis response team." Lean on them. In times of national crisis, the President of the United States calls an emergency meeting of his cabinet. When there are twenty-five seconds on the game clock, the captain of a football team calls a time out and huddles with his players before the final drive. When the bank balance is lean, Dad calls the family together to figure out how to stretch every dollar. And when a church is beset by "fightings and fears within, without," the wise pastor will refuse to go it alone. He or she will recognize the need for teamwork.

Part 2: Crisis Response

Now let's turn to a second response we must make when a ministry storm comes our way.

Chapter 8
Tell the Truth

TALK ABOUT HAVING BIG shoes to fill. How would you like to follow a pastor who had been leading his church for sixty years?

That is the challenge that lay before a twenty-three-year-old Jonathan Edwards in 1729 in Northampton, Massachusetts. Not only had the previous minister, Solomon Stoddard, led Northampton's Congregational Church since 1669, but he was Edwards's maternal grandfather. For two years Edwards had served as Stoddard's pastoral assistant. The death of his beloved mentor left Edwards in charge. To say he rose to the occasion is a gross understatement. From 1729 until 1750 Jonathan Edwards was not only a faithful pastor but came to be regarded as "America's foremost theologian."[1] He went on to serve as a missionary to Native Americans and president of the College of New Jersey before his untimely death in 1758.

Jonathan Edwards's key role in the Great Awakening of the eighteenth century, his sermons (especially "Sinners in the Hands of an Angry God"), his voluminous writings (including *The Life and Diary of David Brainerd*), his rigorous routine of study and meditation, and his eminent progeny are legendary. Edwards's preaching was a primary means by which God brought sweeping revival to the American colonies in the 1730s and 1740s. Tens of thousands of people were converted to Christ—on both sides of

1. Nichols, *Jonathan Edwards*, 25.

PART 2: CRISIS RESPONSE

the Atlantic. The face of religion in America would never be the same.

Not as well known to many are the storms Edwards endured as a pastor.

Epidemics of the late 1740s killed over a tenth of Northampton's population.[2] Edwards's own beloved daughter Jerusha died of an acute fever in 1748. Like ministers today, Edwards was troubled by the lukewarmness, hypocrisy, shallow commitment, and stinginess that characterized some in his congregation. He repeatedly had to ask his elders for a raise. Several powerful, "well-intentioned dragons" in the church maligned him and sought his ruin. Both extremes—the excesses of revivalism as well as the coldness of unconverted hearts—disturbed Edwards. One Sunday morning in 1737 the balcony of his church, filled with worshipers, came crashing down on those seated below. Many were injured, though none killed. There was also a lengthy, divisive controversy in the church about how people should be seated in their new facility. These things caused Edwards sleepless nights and tearful prayers.

Edwards compounded his problems with several unpopular decisions. He refused to visit his congregants in their homes as other pastors were wont to do, preferring to study and counsel serious inquirers out of his house. Frustration with his congregation often leaked out in his sermons. According to historian Douglas Sweeney, Edwards "needled his people incessantly, aggravating his flock."[3] In the "Bad Book Controversy" of 1744, Edwards caused an uproar in Northampton when he came down hard (naming names from the pulpit) on a group of boys who had found a midwife's manual and made lewd comments about it to girls.

Edwards's undoing, however, was the result of his gritty commitment to the truth.

Like other ministers of his day, Edwards's grandfather Stoddard had allowed unconverted people to become members of the church, take the Lord's Supper, and have their children baptized. It was an arrangement called the Halfway Covenant. Edwards

2. Sweeney, *Jonathan Edwards*, 139.
3. Ibid., 138.

rejected that policy as unbiblical. He believed that only those who, "in profession, and in the eye of a reasonable judgment, are truly saints or godly persons" had a right to the signs and seals of the covenant of grace.[4] His effort to reverse the church's policy met with stiff resistance. Leading church members lobbied in opposition to Edwards. He wrote a book explaining his views but hardly anyone read it. The power brokers lined up against him.

Edwards would not change his mind, and on June 22, 1750, he was relieved of his duties.

"The truth will set you free," Jesus said (John 8:32). Jonathan Edwards discovered it can also get you fired. Nevertheless, I have learned that it's always best to be a truth-telling pastor.

During my five years at New Life Church, I was often in situations where I had to make a choice: either tell it like it is and face the consequences, or spin the truth and keep the peace. Too often, I chose the latter option, only to find out that instead of keeping peace it created turmoil.

In chapter 1, I wrote about the worship wars that splintered the church. On one side were those who wanted "contemporary" worship; they were primarily the younger set in the church. On the other side were those who wanted "traditional" worship; they tended to be the older members. Spokespersons of each camp came to me demanding concessions. I reassured each side with promises I could not keep. "Sure, we'll pull out all the stops," I told the contemporary crowd. "Of course we'll sing the old hymns," I promised the traditional crowd. At the time I did not consider that when you fail to qualify such things, people hear what they want to hear and report back to their constituents. Then the story gets spun larger. When you don't deliver as expected, the constituencies demand to know why. If a worship service did not feature a rockin' worship band, the contemporary crowd was upset with me. If a service *did* feature a rockin' worship band, the traditional crowd

---

4. Ibid., 141.

was upset with me. My lack of full disclosure and transparency led to false expectations and anger.

I should have leveled with both sides. I should have said something like this: "Look, we are a church with diverse tastes and preferences. Not everyone will be happy with every worship service. What needs to change is our attitudes. We need to decide that worship is not about drums and guitars or organs and choirs. It's about glorifying God, sitting at his feet, confessing our sins, celebrating the gospel, hearing his Word, and being equipped for mission. In this church we're going to worship God many different ways—some of which you will find foreign to your ears and tastes. We will let the Bible be our guide, not our preferences. And we will work hard to love and respect one another, even when we leave the worship service unfulfilled. Anything less is sinful and doesn't belong at New Life Church."

Sounds simple, right? It's not simple. When power brokers are getting in your face, when people are mad at you, threaten to leave the church, and tell you they wish your church were more like the church down the street, it's tempting to tailor your words to the person or group to whom you're speaking. It's easy to say what you think they want you to say just to keep the peace or get them out of your hair. At that moment of temptation, you need to remember, "Lying lips are an abomination to the Lord, but those who act faithfully are his delight" (Prov 12:22).

Granted, the truth can be spoken brutally. Paul reminds us to speak the truth in love (Eph 4:15). Even if we are angry with someone, we must "sin not" (Eph 4:26). And there are certainly those times when, while telling the truth, we need not tell the *whole* truth. Church members do not need to know everything we know about discipline situations, for example.

But we who tend to be people pleasers will not lead our churches through storms of conflict into brighter days if we let their wishes and whims serve as our north star.

Tell the Truth

Hananiah learned this lesson too late. He was a prophet during the eclipse of the nation of Judah. Evil Zedekiah was on the throne in Jerusalem. He'd been installed as king by Nebuchadnezzar of Babylon, whose armies had besieged the city and led away thousands of Jews to Babylon. Jeremiah the prophet had predicted a seventy-year exile for the people of God. But Hananiah, claiming to speak for God, announced, "Within two years I will bring back to this place all the vessels of the Lord's house, which Nebuchadnezzar king of Babylon took away from this place and carried to Babylon. I will also bring back . . . all the exiles from Judah who went to Babylon, declares the Lord, for I will break the yoke of the king of Babylon" (Jer 28:3–4).

Jeremiah wasn't deceived by Hananiah's flattery. He rebuked Hananiah: "Listen, Hananiah, the Lord has not sent you, and you have made this people trust in a lie. Therefore thus says the Lord: 'Behold, I will remove you from the face of the earth. This year you shall die, because you have uttered rebellion against the Lord'" (Jer 28:15–16). In a matter of weeks, Hananiah was dead.

Telling people what they want to hear often leads to disaster. In chapter 3 I wrote about the Galveston Hurricane of 1900. Isaac Cline was chief meteorologist for the local US Weather Bureau. He had said it was "a crazy idea" that a hurricane would do any serious damage to Galveston. People took his word for it. No one built a seawall for the city's protection. When the hurricane swept through Galveston, Cline nearly drowned; his wife Cora, pregnant with their fourth child, perished in the floodwaters.

In his book *Reflecting the Glory,* N. T. Wright says, "There is always an insidious pressure on a Christian, perhaps particularly on an ordained minister, to go soft on the bits that our hearers might dislike."[5] Pastors are notorious for spin. We inflate attendance numbers, downplay red ink, exaggerate results, and omit negative critiques from our monthly reports to the governing board. We say "I'll pray for you," but have no real intention to do so. We smile and nod to a parishioner while looking over her shoulder at someone we'd prefer to talk to. We underestimate obstacles and overestimate

5. Wright, *Reflecting the Glory,* 27.

the church's ability to overcome them. We proclaim the promises of God's grace but skip the hard calls to obedience and sacrifice. Like the false prophets of old, we often say "Peace, peace," when there is no peace (Jer 6:14).

Ben Franklin was right. "Honesty is the best policy." The integrity we display and the respect we earn through truth telling will be our life jacket in the floodwaters of conflict.

So far my focus in this chapter has been on saying what we mean and meaning what we say. But there's another occasion when a faithful pastor must tell the truth. That is when we need to confront the person or persons causing trouble for our congregation.

Earlier I referred to the "well-intentioned dragons" with whom Jonathan Edwards had to contend. We have author Marshall Shelley to thank for that pithy phrase. His book, *Well-Intentioned Dragons: Ministering to Problem People in the Church*, offers valuable advice for handling difficult church members. Dragons are often "pillars of the community—talented, strong personalities, deservingly respected—but for some reason, they undermine the ministry of the church."[6] They fall into several categories, according to Shelley. There is the Bird Dog, who sniffs around the church looking for things *we* need to take care of. There is the Wet Blanket, who spreads doom and gloom about any initiative we take. There is Captain Bluster, who uses a strong personality to manipulate and control. There is the Fickle Financier, who uses money as leverage to get his or her way. And there are others, like the Busybody, the Sniper, and the Legalist. Name them what you will, all dragons have one thing in common: power—power to destroy enthusiasm, shift responsibility away from themselves, and make you (the pastor) crazy. Some wield their power subtly, through flattery, gifts, promises, and sob stories. Other dragons are more openly hostile, critical, and divisive. Regardless, we must confront them (Matt 18:15–20). This is part of our job "to care for the church of God, which he obtained with his own blood" (Acts 20:28). We cannot

---

6. Shelley, "Identifying a Dragon," 60.

ignore the situation and just hope things will get better. We must let God use us to help these people change. Failing to do so may spare us a painful conversation now, but will hurt our congregation and make life more difficult for us in the long run.

Confronting a disturber of the peace is not something we should do impulsively. Here are seven steps you should take before confronting someone who is causing problems:

1. Pray both for yourself and the person who needs confronting. Ask God to give you a love for that individual and a genuine desire for his or her welfare.

2. Repent of your own sin. Take the log out of your own eye before you try to remove the speck of sawdust out of the other person's eye (Matt 7:5). Identify ways you are like that person. Confess your uncharitable thoughts of him or her.

3. Ask yourself, "What can I learn from this person?" Even your worst critic is telling you something that is at least partly true. How might he or she, with a little help, actually benefit you and the church?

4. Write out what you will say. Begin by asking for permission to speak honestly and openly. Consider opening with, "May I speak from the heart about something that's been bothering me?" or, "Do you agree that one of my roles as a pastor is to bring things to people's attention—sometimes hard things?" Also think of how you can begin on a positive note instead of immediately telling the person where he or she is wrong.

5. Identify and write out the specific changes you expect the person to make. What will repentance look like?

6. Plan out next steps. What will happen if the person refuses to repent? What consequences should he or she expect? What will you do next to assist the person in his or her growth?

7. Call the person and set up a meeting. The sooner the better. Do not put it off or make excuses. The Holy Spirit is prompting you; he will help you. Don't keep him waiting.

Part 2: Crisis Response

Gary McIntosh and Robert Edmondson write, "In every church there is the proverbial squeaky wheel who figures he has a right to as much pastoral 'grease' as he can get."[7] In the course of my ministry I have had to confront quite a few "squeaky wheels." Some of them lived up to the name well-intentioned dragon. I have frequently been surprised by how quickly a dragon can turn into a lamb when rebuked with humble honesty. There have also been times when the conversation did not go so well, and I was singed by hot steam from angry nostrils. But then, I'm a dragon too sometimes. I demand my way with God. I use him and I use people to further my agenda. I can get just as jealous, impatient, controlling, and whiny as the next guy. Thankfully, Jesus came not for the righteous but for sinners like me.

May the Lord empower you through his indwelling Spirit to lead his people with both grace and truth. The truth will set them free.

---

7. McIntosh and Edmondson, *It Only Hurts on Monday*, 161.

Chapter 9
Consult the Experts

MY WIFE AND I recently took two of our grandsons whitewater rafting.

Correction: a skilled guide named Kathryn recently took my wife and me and two of our grandsons whitewater rafting. The Chattooga River in north Georgia is full of rocks, boulders, fallen trees, boils, drops, eddies, hydraulics, falls, and Class IV and V rapids. It would have been sheer lunacy to navigate that river without Kathryn. Even with her in the stern controlling our direction and telling us what to do, we tumbled over a time or two. Without her, we wouldn't have had a clue how to get down that river.

I know what it's like when the winds of dissension, division, betrayal, or some other disturbance start swirling around a church. You don't have a clue. You're feeling a torrent of emotions: confusion, worry, anger, fear, self-loathing, resentment, and guilt. People are disoriented, shouting at each other, not listening. Leaders are saying one thing and then another. Differences you thought were resolved years ago resurface. Emails are flying, tempers are raging, rumors are circulating. Late-night meetings are long, contentious, and unproductive. You've had it up to here with Christians.

Before you lose hope, before you jump overboard—or throw someone else overboard—consider that there may be a skilled guide out there who can get in the boat with you and steer you through the rapids. Someone who's been down this river before, who knows its twists and turns and has the ability to help you and your church survive. Remember chapter 7 about teamwork? That teammate could be available right now, waiting for your call.

Ready for a tragic story?

Pastor James had been at Christ Church for over twenty-four years. You'd think by then his church would be stormproof. But when James started introducing changes to boost the church's outreach, an unseen fault line under Christ Church burst wide open. "We tried to change the culture of the church and it couldn't be done," James told me. "It created inherent tension in the body." Overnight, it seemed, Christ Church took on the air of an intense presidential debate, and James was the political football. The rift unfortunately coincided with the resignations of all five elders. One elder was having marital problems. Another felt he was too old to continue serving. Another resigned to take care of her ailing husband. A fourth elder was diagnosed with bipolar disease and needed hospitalization. The fifth could not abide the changes James was making. So when things were at their most desperate, only James and his assistant pastor were left on the governing board.

An influential couple in the church agreed with James that the church needed to turn its focus outward. For too long, they said, Christ Church had ignored the needs of the community. But when this couple saw a church fight looming, they wanted no part of it; they'd been through that before in another church. So they told James they were leaving. Problem was, that couple contributed nearly a third of Christ Church's offerings. So now, not only was the congregation in turmoil, but it also had little money. The budget had to be slashed; the assistant pastor had to go.

The tension took its toll on James, emotionally and physically. He caught a cold that he could not shake. His teenage daughter said, "Dad, you're under stress." James knew it but didn't know what to do about it. He managed to recruit three new elders from the congregation. They agreed with James theologically but not philosophically. Every board meeting pitted James on one side against the three elders on the other.

"You're taking Christ Church in the wrong direction," they told him.

"You're not listening to the gospel," he replied. It was a stalemate.

Finally, James told his elders what he'd been thinking for months. "We're not a team. It's not good for any of us, and it's not good for the church. Either you need to step down or I need to. If we stay together things are only going to get worse." The elders took offense, as though James was accusing them of fomenting division.

"We're not going anywhere," they told him. So the following Sunday, James announced his resignation.

Three months later, despite their promise to stay, the three elders also left. Absent leadership and with declining membership, Christ Church fell apart and was dissolved by its denomination.

Every year in America, some 3,500 churches shut down.[1] Could Pastor James's church have been spared that fate? Maybe, maybe not. But what if James had called in a couple of experts before things began to go south—like a peacemaking team or a church consultant? The story of Christ Church might have become a story of redemption rather than collapse.

Perhaps you've seen the cable television show, *Intervention*. In each episode, a loving but determined group of family members and friends confront a person trapped in a self-destructive addiction. Guiding the intervention is a professional therapist who has prepared the participants, lays down the rules, and makes sure the encounter goes as well as possible. I'm not comparing (all) church problems to addictions, but you should consider an intervention led by a skilled guide as the appropriate next step in many situations.

---

1. Stetzer and Bird, "US Churches No Longer in Decline," line 2.

Part 2: Crisis Response

My friend Paul Cornwell is co-founder of Crossroads Resolution Group, LLC.[2] Paul provides help when a hurricane of conflict threatens to sabotage a church's ministry. His team includes Christian attorneys, mediators, and counselors. They consult with around fifty churches a year. Paul tells me the most frequent presenting issue in these churches is a loss of trust between pastor and congregation, usually caused by the leader's hurtful behavior and/or inability to know how to apply the gospel to the conflict. He says that while these leaders have a general knowledge of biblical peacemaking (e.g., Matt 18), they fail to apply such principles effectively. Rather than getting underneath the storm to the causative issues, they focus on a checklist approach to resolving conflict. Crossroads Resolution Group can help pastors lower their defenses, identify their own heart idols, communicate more effectively, and partner with others to build a culture of peace in their church.

A similar organization, Peacemaker Ministries, has been offering conflict coaching, mediation, and arbitration for over thirty-five years.[3] In a church I once served, a storm erupted that was as complicated as it was explosive. My elders and I spent countless hours listening to the parties involved and trying to tiptoe through the minefield. It was the most confusing and emotionally taxing situation I've ever encountered as a pastor. I spent many days and nights praying, crying, talking, and trying to figure out what to do next. Someone told me about Peacemaker Ministries. To make a long story short, we hired a pair of their trained conciliators to take us through a biblical, carefully supervised process that eventually brought resolution. We lost a few members because of the conflict, but without Peacemaker's help the fallout would have been much worse.

Maybe your situation does not warrant the services of a professional conciliator. Nevertheless, you could turn for advice to others, such as:

- Another pastor

2. http://crossroadsresolution.com
3. http://peacemaker.net

CONSULT THE EXPERTS

- A licensed mental health counselor
- A church consultant
- Someone at your denominational headquarters who assists church leaders
- One of your old seminary professors
- The author of a book or article that addresses your situation
- An older member of your church known for his or her wisdom
- A retired pastor or missionary
- Your parents
- Your spouse[4]

When things were crashing around me at New Life Church, besides meeting with fellow leaders and talking to my wife I did three things that were of inestimable value. First, I called a pastor in a nearby city and told him everything that was happening. I asked him to come to our next elder board meeting and help bring a truce to the worship wars. This pastor was older than I and had a reputation as a calm pragmatist and loving listener. He traveled 140 miles on three different occasions to assist my elders and me.

Second, I called our church's denominational offices and asked to talk to someone who understood conflict resolution. I figured they had to have been down this kind of Class V rapid before me. I discovered that two people were employed by my denomination for the precise purpose of assisting churches in turmoil. They traveled to my church and spent a week on site interviewing church members, leaders, and staff. The report they left us contained both

---

4. If you assume every married pastor talks with his or her mate about church matters, you are likely surprised that I include your spouse on this list. Some pastors prefer to leave their work in their briefcase or office rather than bring it home to their family. Others share scant details with their spouse in order to protect him or her from animus toward church members. But when dealing with conflict or making hard decisions, your spouse can give you the very best advice on the planet.

a helpful assessment of the church and recommendations that proved beneficial. And their services were free.

The third step I took was arranging marriage counseling for my wife and me. Our therapist's office was in the next county, which added a sense of privacy to our counseling sessions. Church turmoil exacts a mighty toll upon a marriage. The value of pouring our hearts out to a well-trained counselor, being reminded of God's unconditional love and gaining a disinterested person's perspective on our situation cannot be exaggerated.

When I say consult the experts, I am not implying that they are necessarily better than the anointed leaders of a congregation or that those leaders should abdicate their responsibility to shepherd the church through seasons of pain. The call to "maintain the unity of the Spirit in the bond of peace" applies in the first place to those shepherds on the ground (Eph 4:3). Even when it is both physically and emotionally draining, the leaders of a church must keep watch over the souls of their church members. One day they "will have to give an account" of their stewardship (Heb 13:17).

But sometimes they are too close to the situation, too emotionally involved in it, to see things objectively. Besides, does not Scripture call us to welcome counsel?

- "Without counsel plans fail, but with many advisers they succeed" (Prov 15:22).
- "Where there is no guidance, a people falls, but in an abundance of counselors there is safety" (Prov 11:14).
- ". . . [B]y wise guidance you can wage your war, and in abundance of counselors there is victory" (Prov 24:6).
- "The way of a fool is right in his own eyes, but a wise man listens to advice" (Prov 12:15).

God has equipped many people to serve the church from outside its walls. Wise pastors avail themselves of their skills. My website[5] features a list of books, articles, websites, retreats, and other resources to help pastors navigate the turbulent waters of

---

5. www.survivingministry.com

church conflict. With so many helps and people available to assist, no church leader should brave the whitewater alone.

It must be said, however, that sometimes even the best outside expert cannot navigate a wild river of discord. You might have to take more drastic measures. In the case of New Life Church, the continual wrangling over worship styles led us to conclude that a "splant" was called for (to remind you, that's a split cleverly disguised as a church plant). If the Hatfields and McCoys would not get along, we would start a new church for the Hatfields. So we sent the youth pastor and worship leader to a new location and gave the group a new name. About two-thirds of the congregation went with them. The Cat 5 winds died down immediately, but my vision and energy for leadership were shot. Within six months after the splant, I was gone.

One of the main lessons I learned from this painful experience is the subject of the next chapter.

Chapter 10
Pick Your Battles

DURING A HURRICANE, SOME battles are worth fighting and others are not. If you had been living on the Gulf Coast during Hurricane Katrina, the length of your daughter's skirt, the loss on your latest investment, and the damage being done by squirrels in your attic would suddenly be of no concern. All you would care about is getting yourself and your loved ones to higher ground. Hurricanes have a way of redefining *important*.

The same is true in the church during times of turmoil. Some battles are worth fighting and others are not. Knowing the difference is a mark of pastoral wisdom.

I know a minister who fought many battles. Once he told a ministry partner to take a hike because the man had befriended someone with a dubious track record (Acts 15:36–41). Another time he publicly embarrassed a prominent fellow minister for his hypocrisy (Gal 2:11–14). He sometimes wrote scathing letters exposing doctrinal error and loose morals. He went on several mission trips where his life was in danger and refused offers of safety. He boldly preached the gospel in spite of death threats, physical attack, arrest, and imprisonment. Of course I'm talking about the apostle Paul. Paul had decided that a few key hills are worth dying on. He often jumped into the fray, risking comfort, safety, and reputation. Were those battles worth fighting? Two thousand years of church history say yes.

PICK YOUR BATTLES

But then sometimes the apostle strategically decided that deference was better than controversy. He circumcised his young protégé Timothy in Asia Minor rather than offend the Jews he was seeking to win (Acts 16:1–3). He moonlighted as a tentmaker rather than be a financial burden on churches (Acts 18:1–3, 1 Thess 2:9). When falsely accused, he followed proper legal channels to establish his innocence (Acts 25:8–12). When under arrest he repented for speaking words of disrespect to the high priest Ananias (Acts 23:1–5). While in prison he rejoiced that even those motivated by selfish rivalry were preaching the gospel (Phil 1:12–18). Paul knew when to dig in his heels over principle and when not to.

Several times a day pastors have a choice to make: "Is this a hill to die on or not? Whether I fight or let it go, what will be the consequences of my decision?" Some issues are far weightier than others. Choosing a new pen for the pew racks in the sanctuary is one thing; deciding whether you should perform the wedding of a gay couple is another. Depending on your denominational or theological tradition, some matters are not even up for discussion. But often the battle lines are not so easy to discern. Plus, the blood that may get spilled on the floor is that of real people, not concepts.

In one church I served, a storm erupted around a staff member I'll call Bethany (not her real name). She was the director of our women's ministry. Bethany was popular with many of our ladies and teenage girls. She had a heart for the lonely and downtrodden. She held women in rapt attention as she taught Bible studies. But from the day I met Bethany, my gut said something did not quite line up. As time went on, I observed that she would smile and nod when I asked her to do certain things, then either fail to carry out my instructions or do the opposite. The accolades given her by some women were too extreme to be healthy. She thrived on attention and boasted about her influence on others. She would sneak not-so-subtle critiques of church leaders into her conversations with other women. Ladies started giving me reports of inconsistencies and outright slander coming from Bethany's lips, while an equal number rallied around her. I met with Bethany and made my dissatisfaction clear. Either the inappropriate behavior would stop or she would need to look for another job. Some of her supporters came to me and spoke in her defense. Other women, however, saw her as a saboteur. If I fired Bethany, I knew I would face the wrath of her fan club; they already felt women were marginalized in our church. But if I did not fire her, Bethany would undermine the peace and purity of the church. It was a battle I had to fight, win or lose. I fired Bethany because you just can't put up with staff members who work against the team. Interestingly, a few weeks after her dismissal the furor was over. Even the fan club realized the damage Bethany had been causing the church.

We cannot run from battles caused by bad hires, staff insubordination, and sin in the camp. These things can and do rip churches apart. Read through the book of Nehemiah. There you'll see an example of a leader whose love for God and God's people compelled him to take action against injustice and sin. Nehemiah followed the maxim attributed to President Ronald Reagan: "When you can't make them see the light, make them feel the heat."

However, every issue in the church does not require us to put on our boxing gloves. We might win the battle and find out later we were on the wrong side of the issue. Time has a way of changing things after all, including convictions. Or we might lose. Not all wars are winnable, as the pages of history attest. All storms eventually pass. In some situations, the best response to a church hurricane is to hunker down, hold on, cherish our loved ones, preach the gospel, and be patient. Paul's reminder to "be patient in tribulation" (Rom 12:12) is valuable advice to pastors whose churches are in turmoil. Not every difference of opinion in the church deserves to become a duel.

Have you noticed how often the phrase "wait for the Lord" appears in the book of Psalms? Here is a sampling:

- "I wait for the Lord, my soul waits, and in his word I hope; my soul waits for the Lord more than watchmen for the morning, more than watchmen for the morning" (Ps 130:5–6).

- "I waited patiently for the Lord; he inclined to me and heard my cry" (Ps 40:1).
- "Wait for the Lord; be strong, and let your heart take courage; wait for the Lord!" (Ps 27:14).
- "Be strong, and let your heart take courage, all you who wait for the Lord!" (Ps 31:24).
- "Wait for the Lord and keep his way, and he will exalt you to inherit the land; you will look on when the wicked are cut off" (Ps 37:34).

With all these (and more) biblical commands to wait on God, we who tend to make a knee-jerk response to stress would do well to spend at least some time waiting on our Commander-in-Chief for direction.

But let's suppose you've been at your church for three or four years. You've earned enough capital to begin proposing significant changes. The church is mostly made up of aging Baby Boomers and Builders. The number of families with children and teens has been on a sharp decline for years. You have just a handful of young single adults. Yet the surrounding community is bursting with Millennials and Gen Xers. You've done a lot of work to understand the church's story and the needs of the community. You're concerned about the future of the church. You believe it's time to change the name of the church, introduce a Saturday night contemporary worship service, and hire a children's director. Your leaders are on board. It should be a fairly easy sell.

But when you tell the congregation your ideas, you unleash a hurricane-force storm:

- "We built this church thirty-five years ago. What do you mean you want to change the name of the church?"
- "We spend too much money on staff already. You want to add another staff member? Recruit a volunteer to minister to our kids."

PART 2: CRISIS RESPONSE

- "Contemporary worship is not worship. Young people need to sing the old hymns."
- "Don't the needs of us older people matter? You don't care about us."

Obviously, you have touched a nerve. A portion of the congregation does not agree that your renewal program is brilliant. Guerrilla warfare begins. Small groups gather after the worship service to talk in low tones about you. They like things the way they are. They feel left out of the process. The church is going the way of the world, they say. You're surrendering the church's distinctives, they say. Maybe they'll circulate a petition. Maybe they'll ask for an open meeting with the governing board. Maybe they'll shop around for another church.

What do you do? Is this a battle you should fight? If you do, will you win? And what might winning the battle cost you?

Consultant and author André Bustanoby fought in the Air Force during the Korean conflict. Drawing from his experience in the military, Bustanoby says there are some wars you will not win and probably should not fight. "There are times," he writes, "when we should turn over scorched earth to determined terrorists."[1] He recommends that you answer these seven questions before engaging in combat:

- Does the church have a history of driving pastors away?
- Have your efforts to achieve peace in the past repeatedly failed?
- Are your leaders prepared to pay the price of victory?
- Is there a critical mass of support in the congregation?
- Is the opposition willing to negotiate, or do they demand unconditional surrender?
- How will fighting the battle affect your family?

---

1. Bustanoby, "Wars You Can't Win," 222.

Pick Your Battles

- Why fight? Is it to benefit your church and community or satisfy your personal need to win?[2]

In the hypothetical case we are considering, let's say you decide to fight but you split your proposal into two parts. The name change is not as important as hiring a children's director and starting a Saturday night service. So you decide to put that idea on the back burner or drop it altogether. That's not a hill you're willing to die on. But you believe if the church is ever to reach a younger demographic, updating your worship style and investing in children are critical. Your research found that many singles and young families are busy on Sunday with work, travel, or children's activities. College students typically sleep in on Sunday. That's why a Saturday night service makes sense. This church does not have a history of driving pastors away. It's been a unified, biblically-minded church filled with people who have walked with God for a long time. Your wife and your leaders are behind you; they are as convinced as you are that you're on the right track. You have done a heart check and concluded you're not seeking your own glory; it's the future of the church that concerns you. You don't know if your opponents are willing to negotiate, but you'll take the risk. You decide to hold a series of open discussions with your disgruntled members to listen to them and help them understand why you believe those changes are good for the kingdom of God. By nondefensively hearing their fears and concerns, meeting one on one with influencers, and communicating your vision in a clear, consistent way, you hope they will see your proposals in a different light. It seems a winnable war, though there's no guarantee. You pray for God's blessing and plunge forward.

There are ways to change things without a fight.

The church I currently serve advocates small groups. We tell people that if they are not in a small group, they will not experience the kind of shepherding and community that are essential for discipleship. We also ascribe to the theory that as the number

[2]. Ibid., 210–222.

of church programs goes up, ministry effectiveness goes down. We agree with Thom Rainer and Eric Geiger, who argue in their book *Simple Church*, ". . . in order to be focused, you must be careful not to add programs to the ministry process. Doing so would lengthen it; and the longer it is, the fewer people will be able to move through it. It will be an ongoing battle."[3]

Over sixty percent of our congregation are in small groups. That's pretty good, but we'd like to see that percentage go way up. We have identified our adult Sunday school program as a potential threat to the small group ministry. In our busy city, most adults have enough time for just one or two church activities besides the weekly worship service. If a choice has to be made, we'd rather they be in a small group than attend a Sunday school class. We believe a small group is a better venue for community and spiritual growth than a lecture-oriented class. So in a recent congregational meeting I said that the leadership is considering shutting down the adult Sunday school program. You would think I had announced the closing of the local Starbucks. A collective moan came from the audience. I pointed out how relatively few adults attend Sunday school. It didn't matter. Shutting down a Sunday school program is, in many minds, the first step down the slippery slope to paganism.

Our leaders could fight this battle over Sunday school. We could kill the program and insist that our members join a small group if it's spiritual growth they're after. Or we could get to our desired destination by another route. Many church leaders have found that if you want a program to die, just don't invest in it. Don't keep propping it up. Let it die of neglect, and put your energy where it will do the most good.

And that's what we've decided to do. We're not canceling the adult Sunday school program. That's not a battle we want to fight. But we're also not going to spend time recruiting teachers, putting out promos, buying materials, staffing it, and planning ways for it to succeed. We're simply going to provide space for interested persons, let them select a Bible-based video series, and get out of

---

3. Rainer and Geiger, *Simple Church*, 210.

their way. We'll devote our energy to creating the best small group program we possibly can. In time, the adult Sunday school program will—with God's blessing—fade into oblivion.

Some battles *must* be fought. It's my conviction that followers of Jesus must go to the mat for the inerrancy of Scripture; the value of human life at all stages of development; the sanctity of lifelong marriage between a man and a woman; the primacy of the church and of the family; the virgin birth, sinless life, vicarious death, bodily resurrection, triumphant ascension, and future glorious return of Jesus Christ; the universality of sin; the necessity of spiritual rebirth; the gospel of salvation by grace alone through faith alone in Christ alone; the certainty of future judgment and the eternal state; the priority of evangelism; and the triune nature of the Godhead. These, for me, are "closed hand" doctrines. I will not surrender or retreat on those matters. At the end of my life I want to be able to say with Paul, "I have fought the good fight, I have finished the race, I have kept the faith" (2 Tim 4:7).

Other doctrines, while vitally important, are "open hand" doctrines. I cherish the distinctives of my Presbyterian tradition but will freely admit I may be wrong about this or that particular. I will not fight to the death on doctrines like infant baptism and Presbyterian polity; my Baptist friends have good, biblical arguments for their beliefs, just as I do. When it comes to controversies and strife in the church, a wise pastor will weigh the benefits and costs before picking a fight.

Is there one crisis response that is more important than any other? You guessed it. Let's turn our attention to prayer.

Chapter 11
Pray

IT SEEMED LIKE A great idea at the time.

Brent and Mario, both in their late twenties, had been friends since they were teenagers. They both desired to see the gospel spread in their part of the city. They had talked and prayed about planting a church together for a long time. So what if they didn't have the funding or oversight of a denomination. So what if they had no church planting experience. They had teaching and preaching gifts. They could do this, no sweat. So the two found space for rent in a well-traveled part of the city. They contacted friends who promised to help get the church off the ground. They spread the word and started up a worship service. People came, and they liked what they saw. Attendance grew week after week. Mario and Brent split up the preaching. Mario, ever the entrepreneur, set his sights on strong, steady growth. Brent, the artistic one, valued strong relationships in the church. It seemed like a complementary team.

But soon, according to Brent, "things got strange" between him and Mario. Brent sensed a rift developing between him and his friend. Then one day about six months in, Mario announced, "This is how it's going to be, Brent. I'm going to be the lead pastor. I've been to seminary and you haven't. I know how to raise funds. You really need more training. So I'm going to get paid by the church and you're not. I need your help as a volunteer but you'll need to keep your day job."

Brent was astonished. Mario had figured all this out without ever talking to him. Mario had even put together an advisory team, and they approved the plan. Brent didn't like it but he didn't want to fight his friend. Maybe Mario was right. Maybe he did need more training. So he took Mario's advice and enrolled in a nearby seminary. He continued serving the church in a variety of ways.

Months went by. Then one day, out of nowhere, Mario announced he'd hired an associate pastor. It was a cruel slap in the face to Brent. He had no idea this was happening. The two friends stopped talking altogether. Brent says, "It was painful. Something was way off."

Late one evening Terry, the new associate pastor, gave Brent a call. "We need to talk," he said. Brent and Terry met the next morning at a coffee shop. "Mario has been plagiarizing other people's sermons," Terry told him. "And it's been going on for a long time."

"No way." Brent said. But Terry showed him example after example of Mario's plagiarism. They knew they needed to confront Mario. "It was the worst meeting I've ever experienced," Brent told me. Mario was hostile, angry, unwilling to admit his sin. Instead of repenting, he said he would just resign his post and leave the church. Brent and Terry went to the elders and told them what Mario had been doing and how he'd reacted. Hoping for damage control, the elders explained to the congregation the following Sunday that Mario was going to resign over "philosophical differences." But the people knew better. Something more serious had come between two good friends.

The little church was now two years old and without a lead pastor. Because Brent had been there from the beginning, the elders asked him to step up and lead the church. But one after another, disillusioned people left the church. Even the core group, Brent's closest friends, decided it was time to go. Brent did his best for the next three years, but attendance and giving went steadily downhill. Outreach efforts went nowhere. The church was down to forty people. It felt like a house church meeting in a big building. Brent grew more and more exhausted. He was working, going to seminary, and trying to raise a sinking ship all at the same time.

Part 2: Crisis Response

Some days he came home so discouraged he wished he were dead. Fortunately, his marriage and family were healthy, but his church was on life support.

Brent prayed, "Lord, I feel like a total failure. Is this really what you intend for this church? Do you want it to die—and crush me in the process? I thought this is what I was created to do. Was I wrong?"

The good news is that Brent is now the lead pastor of a church in another city. He is recovering from his ministry hurricane and his congregation is doing great. But when his church plant was bleeding members, he was a mess. He felt he was to blame for the church's decline. Mario had said Brent "needed more training." Maybe what Mario was implying was that Brent wasn't qualified to be a minister of the gospel. Maybe his preaching was defective; maybe he had no business being a pastor; maybe he was really a failure as a leader, as a man. Such are the thoughts that spiral downward in the minds of many pastors when things go haywire in their church.

Brent came close to throwing in the towel. But he did not. Instead, he chose to hang on to God, and to hope, through prayer. The fact that today he has a renewed vision for pastoral ministry is a tribute to the power of prayer and the grace of a prayer-hearing God.

As a Presbyterian, I hold the Westminster Shorter Catechism, penned in England in the mid-1600s, to be a faithful summary of the Bible's teaching on a range of subjects. Christians of many traditions have memorized the answer to Question 1 which asks, "What is the chief end of man?" The answer: "Man's chief end is to glorify God, and to enjoy him forever." The catechism's last section deals with the topic of prayer. Question 98 asks, "What is prayer?" The answer is, "Prayer is an offering up of our desires unto God, for things agreeable to his will, in the name of Christ, with confession of our sins, and thankful acknowledgment of his mercies."

Notice that the Westminster divines defined prayer essentially as "an offering up of our desires unto God." It would seem that nothing could be simpler and more natural for Christians than telling their heavenly Father their desires. Yet many believers I talk to say that prayer is their greatest struggle in their walk with God. Some of us do not pray at all save in times of emergency. Or if we pray, we don't enjoy praying. It's a burden rather than a blessing, a duty rather than a delight.

But the language of prayer is *desire*. Our passions, our aspirations, our hopes and dreams are the stuff of prayer. When Jesus taught his disciples the Lord's Prayer, his intent was not that they should mindlessly mouth the words, "Our Father in heaven, hallowed be your name, your kingdom come, your will be done on earth . . . ," but instead that they would use the prayer as a tool to express their inmost desires and yearnings to God (Matt 6:5–15).

If prayer is to become not our last resort but our first recourse in times of church turmoil, I suggest we need to understand two things about our desires.

First, our desires are valid. Followers of Jesus have aspirations that are good, holy, and righteous. That's what the Bible says. "Delight yourself in the Lord," wrote David, "and he will give you the desires of your heart" (Ps 37:4). Some interpreters say this means God will give us new desires—desires we didn't have before. That goes without saying, but it's not what the verse says. The sense is rather, "He will give you what your heart longs for." David also wrote, "[God] fulfills the desire of those who fear him" (Ps 145:19).

Think about two stories from the life of Jesus. One day Jesus was walking down the road from Jericho to Jerusalem when he came upon two blind men. When they heard Jesus was approaching, they cried out, "Lord, have mercy on us, Son of David!" The crowd tried to quiet the blind men. But they shouted all the more loudly, "Lord, have mercy on us, Son of David!" Jesus stopped, went over to the two men, and asked, "What do you want me to do for you?" (Matt 20:29–34). In other words, "What do you desire?" On another occasion Jesus was in Jerusalem visiting a pool called Bethesda. "A multitude of invalids" used to lie around this pool because they believed it contained healing powers. The blind, the lame, and the diseased were there. Jesus took particular interest in one old man who had been coming to that pool for thirty-eight years. He was a helpless paralytic. His body was all shriveled up. Jesus stepped over to the poor man and asked, "Do you want to be healed?" (John 5:2–15).

Now why would Jesus ask such ridiculous questions? Wouldn't he know the blind men wanted to see? Didn't he know the old man by the pool of Bethesda wanted to get well? Of course he did. Jesus asked these questions to help these men feel, own, and express their yearnings to him. Similarly, Jesus asks you every day a ridiculously simple question: "What do you want me to do for you today? What do you need? What are you yearning for today in your marriage, your family, your church, your neighborhood, your city? What's the daily bread you need me to give you?"

If I were to answer Jesus right now as I write this paragraph, I would tell him the following: "Jesus, I feel pretty lonely. It's been a long time since I had a meal and a conversation with a good male friend—someone with whom I can totally be myself. I desire that, Jesus. That's my daily bread right now."

Ah, that felt good.

Don't ignore your desires. God wants you to identify them, accept them, and express them. They are valid.

Second, desires help us pray. That should be obvious from what I just said.

Some of us don't enjoy our prayer life because we're always praying for things we think we *should* pray for instead of things we really feel and *want* to pray for. Earlier in my life I tried to devise a system for praying. I made a list of the days of the week, and next to each day I wrote down names of people and things for which I would pray. It looked great on paper. But after a couple of weeks my prayer life once again sputtered and died. To be perfectly honest, I just did not always *want* to pray for those items on those particular days.

Think about some of the people in the Bible who were women and men of prayer. Their prayers bear the stamp of spontaneity and need.

- In Genesis 32, Jacob was on his way home with his wives and children after fourteen years of absence. He would soon meet Esau who, he imagined, was quite angry with him. Jacob was afraid. He spent the night alone by a river. The text says a man wrestled with him till daybreak. It was the angel of the Lord. The angel said to Jacob, "Let me go, for the day has broken." But Jacob said, "I will not let you go unless you bless me" (Gen 32:22–32).

When was the last time you prayed, "God, I won't let you go unless you bless me"?

- In Exodus 33, Moses was bone-weary. He had come down from Mt. Sinai with the tablets of the law in his hands only to find the Israelites worshiping a golden calf. He had interceded for the people and God had relented from totally destroying them. Then Moses went outside the camp to the tent of meeting and prayed in desperation, "Please, show me your glory. I can't lead these people to the Promised Land until you show me your glory" (Exod 33:12–23).

When were you so disappointed or overwhelmed by the responsibilities of ministry that you cried out, "Father, show me your glory. I can't go another day in ministry unless you show me your glory"?

Again and again in the Bible, God's people turned desire into prayer. The book of Psalms is full of the language of desire:

- Arise, O Lord! Save me, O my God! For you strike all my enemies on the cheek; you break the teeth of the wicked (Ps 3:7).
- My soul . . . is greatly troubled. But you, O Lord—how long? Turn, O Lord, deliver my life; save me for the sake of your steadfast love . . . I am weary with my moaning; every night I

flood my bed with tears; I drench my couch with my weeping (Ps 6:3, 4, 6).

- I say to God, my rock: "Why have you forgotten me? Why do I go mourning because of the oppression of the enemy?" As with a deadly wound in my bones, my adversaries taunt me, while they say to me all the day long, "Where is your God?" (Ps 42:9–10).

When Daniel found out that Jerusalem would lie in ruins for seventy years, he turned his face to the Lord, "seeking him by prayer and pleas for mercy with fasting and sackcloth and ashes" (Dan 9:3). When Jeremiah received word from God that the land of Judah would become a waste because of sin, he wailed, "Oh that my head were waters, and my eyes a fountain of tears, that I might weep day and night for the slain of the daughter of my people!" (Jer 9:1). When Paul felt concern for the churches he had planted, he prayed for them: "I do not cease . . . remembering you in my prayers," he told the church in Ephesus (Eph 1:16). "[W]e have not ceased to pray for you, asking that you may be filled with the knowledge of [God's] will," he told the Colossians (Col 1:9). "[W]e always pray for you, that our God may make you worthy of his calling," he told the Thessalonians (2 Thess 1:11).

I don't believe Paul was lying when he said that he prayed constantly. How was it possible? It was possible because he really cared about these people. He desired their spiritual growth. One time he told a group of people that he was "in the anguish of childbirth" for their spiritual formation (Gal 4:19). These people weren't just names on a list.

Our Savior prayed out his desires. "In the days of his flesh, Jesus offered up prayers and supplications, with loud cries and tears, to him who was able to save him from death . . . " (Heb 5:7). In the wilderness, on the mountainside, by the tomb of Lazarus, in Gethsemane, and of course, on the cross Jesus offered up his desires unto God for things agreeable to his will. How wonderful that when our Lord prayed on Calvary, "Father, forgive them, for they know not what they do," it was no perfunctory request from a prayer list but the ardent desire of his merciful heart that we be saved (Luke 23:34).

It is true that God does not always grant our desires. Remember Paul's thorn in the flesh? Three times Paul pleaded with God to take it away. He wanted to be free of it. But God said, "No, Paul. My grace will be sufficient for you" (2 Cor 12:7–10). Though God sometimes says no, he invites our sincere, unedited prayers. We can pray our fears, our worries, our sorrows, our anger, our disappointment, our hopes, our dreams, and our wants, and leave the results up to our wise and good Father. E. M. Bounds, who wrote at least nine books on prayer, said,

> Without desire, prayer is a meaningless mumble of words. Such perfunctory, formal praying, with no heart, no feeling, no real desire accompanying it, is to be shunned like a pestilence. Its exercise is a waste of precious time, and from it, no real blessing accrues.[1]

Why are many of us pastors reluctant to take our uncensored desires to God in prayer? It may be due to bad teaching we've received. That teaching goes something like this: "It's not appropriate to express your desires. Desires are evil. Good Christians should be content with what they have. Good Christians don't want things. They're just glad they have anything at all."

It is true that we should be content. It is also true that some desires are evil. Sometimes I want to cuss somebody out. Sometimes I want my neighbor's new car. Paul told Timothy to "Flee youthful passions" (2 Tim 2:22). Peter says, "As obedient children, do not be confirmed to the passions of your former ignorance" (1 Pet 1:14). James warns us that selfish desires cause quarrels and fights: "You desire and do not have, so you murder. You covet and cannot obtain, so you fight and quarrel" (Jas 4:1–2). We should repent of desires that are idolatrous and hurtful to others. But as sons and daughters of God, we have the Holy Spirit inside us. We are new people, with new desires. Paul says that we "who live

---

1. Bounds, *Necessity of Prayer*, lines 7–8.

according to the Spirit set [our] minds on the things of the Spirit" (Rom 8:5). We have a new orientation to please God and seek his kingdom. We have good and godly passions and goals. We care about the things of God.

So listen to your desires and tell God about them. Even if they are evil desires, there are often godly desires hiding underneath. Take them to the throne and tell your Father about them. Don't bottle them up inside. After all, Jesus is asking you, "What do you want me to do for you?"

When a storm of dissension, division, or disorder hits the church, prayer is often the last thing on our minds. We are more prone to respond to crisis with panicked activity than with thoughtful prayer. But now let's talk about a response that is even harder than praying: listening.

Chapter 12
Listen

LIKE MANY AMERICAN CITIES in the late 1980s and early '90s, Boston's violent crime rate soared. The city was struggling to remedy gun violence. Usually drug-related, it often caused the deaths of young men who were in the wrong place at the wrong time. There were twenty-two youth homicides in 1987 and seventy-three in 1990—an increase of 230 percent. Between 1991 and 1995, Boston averaged about forty-four youth homicides a year.[1] But then something amazing happened. By 1998 violent crime in Boston had declined by nearly eighty percent. Between 1997 and 2000 there were fewer than twenty youth homicides each year.[2]

It's been called the Boston Miracle.

What accounts for it? Much of the credit goes to the Boston Police Department and their new tactics for dealing with gangs. But if it had not been for Pastor Jeffrey Brown the miracle might never have happened and the violent crime rate in Boston might have continued to escalate.

Reverend Jeffrey Brown was pastor of Union Baptist Church in Cambridge. As he tells the story,[3] he was preaching sermons and creating church-based programs in hopes of appealing to the

1. Wikipedia, s.v. "Operation Ceasefire," line 5.
2. Bass and Borgman, "The Boston Miracle," lines 9–10.
3. Brown, "How We Cut Youth Violence in Boston by 79 Percent." TED Talk, March 2015.

at-risk youth of inner-city neighborhoods like Roxbury, Dorchester, and Mattapan. But they were not responding. He tried volunteering at the local high schools, but he discovered the kids he needed to reach weren't in school. It took the death of a teenager just a stone's throw away from his church to propel Pastor Brown into a new kind of action. He realized he needed to go outside the walls of his church and build relationships directly with those committing the acts of violence.

He contacted several other area ministers and asked them to partner with him. Night after night, Pastor Brown and his new colleagues walked the most dangerous streets of Boston's inner-city neighborhoods between 10:00 p.m. and 3:00 a.m. Their purpose was neither to exploit the violent youth nor condemn or get them arrested, but to do something much more radical: listen.

Brown and his fellow ministers asked questions, listened, and learned. "Help us understand what life is like on the streets," they said. "What are we not seeing? How do you see the church helping this situation? How can we work together?"

Imagine that: a group of preachers not preaching but listening. It must have been quite a sight, these "reverends," some wearing collars, walking inner-city streets and meeting drug dealers, prostitutes, gang leaders, and potential killers.

From these nighttime encounters came the TenPoint Coalition, an ecumenical group of Christian leaders working together to mobilize the community around issues affecting young blacks and Latinos. Then the Boston Police Department collaborated with the church leaders in an initiative called Operation Ceasefire. Arrests and prosecutions went down. More emphasis was placed on conversation, respect, drug treatment, mediated gang truces, and job placement. The violent crime rate began to decrease dramatically. According to a 2001 report by the US Department of Justice, "the implementation of Operation Ceasefire was associated with a 63-percent decrease in youth homicides per month, a 32-percent decrease in shots-fired calls for service per month, a 25-percent decrease in gun assaults per month, and a 44-percent decrease in the number of youth gun assaults per month in the highest risk district (Roxbury)."[4]

Since its success in Boston, the Operation Ceasefire strategy has been replicated in over sixty cities nationwide. Gun violence among American youth, while a perennial problem, is declining—thanks to a small group of pastors who took time to listen.

Human beings find it incredibly hard to listen to each other. God created us with two ears and only one mouth, yet talking is a lot easier than listening. We live in a noisy world. Places of calm and quiet are few and far between. Images and sounds constantly crisscross our eyes and ears. Communication devices and entertainment media fill up the empty spaces and leave little room for a calm chat with a friend. My wife and I were in a local restaurant a few days ago trying to have a conversation. I counted fourteen television screens mounted on the wall around us, each streaming a sports event or the latest national news. Music by Mumford and Sons was on the loudspeakers. A rowdy bunch of male twenty-somethings were in the booth next to us. Patrons and servers were constantly walking past our table. No wonder I can't remember a single thing we talked about.

Listening is especially difficult when you're convinced you're right. Pastors go to seminary to become right. We are paid to be right. Furthermore, most of us have pretty big egos; we know we're right. So when dissent, disagreement, and debate create turmoil in the church, our natural reaction is to tell people what to do. The way we look at it, if they would just accept the new worship style, vote yes on the new building plan, keep their opinion about the Bible version we are using to themselves, or sign up for the evangelism class, all would be well. But sit down with our opponents and listen to them? That's the last thing we want to do. And if it looks like we're listening, we're really formulating our next killer comeback that will put the matter to rest.

---

4. Kennedy, et al., *Reducing Gun Violence*, 4.

Part 2: Crisis Response

Listening is a must for followers of Christ. Over thirty times in the book of Jeremiah alone, God either exhorts his people to listen to him or rebukes them for not listening. Nearly fifteen times in the book of Proverbs, God affirms the value of listening to his words, a parent's instruction, or a life-giving reproof. Five times in the book of Deuteronomy God says through Moses, "Hear, O Israel." Five times in the gospels Jesus says, "He who has ears to hear, let him hear." The apostle James exhorts his readers, "[L]et every person be quick to hear, slow to speak, slow to anger" (Jas 1:19) All these and other reminders in the Bible serve to underscore both the importance and the difficulty of being a listener instead of a talker.

Jesus was the best listener that ever lived. I cannot imagine that he even once interrupted someone.

Let me be practical. I have taught perhaps hundreds of people the skill of active listening. Active listening involves tuning in completely to what another person is saying and feeling. Instead of interrupting, apologizing, denying, arguing, defending yourself, formulating a response, or proposing a solution, you simply reflect or bounce back what you are hearing from the other person. Active listening is hard work. You have to focus on the other person's words, eyes, body language, and tone of voice, and tune out everything else—including your own opinions. You have to resist the temptation to dismiss what the other person is telling you or fight back with words. Your own ideas go to the back burner, at least for a while.

To illustrate active listening, imagine that a disgruntled church member named Jane comes to her pastor with a complaint:

Example A - Without Active Listening

JANE. Why haven't you visited my mother in the hospital? She feels no one cares about her. I know she's not a member of the church but I am, and my mother has had a serious operation. A lot of people in the church feel you are not concerned enough about the sick.

LISTEN

PASTOR. Jane, really. Do you not understand how busy I am? I'm not able to see everyone in the hospital. That's just not realistic. It's everyone's job to visit the sick, not just mine.

JANE. Maybe you're *too* busy then, Pastor. As a member of this church I think it's reasonable to expect you to make time for hospital visits. Maybe I don't belong in this church anymore.

PASTOR. I'm sorry you feel that way. I'm doing the best I can. OK look, I'll get by the hospital tomorrow. Will that make you feel better?

Example B - With Active Listening

JANE. Why haven't you visited my mother in the hospital? She feels no one cares about her. I know she's not a member of the church but I am, and my mother has had a serious operation. A lot of people in the church feel you are not concerned enough about the sick.

PASTOR. You're upset that I haven't visited your mom in the hospital.

JANE. Yes, I'm hurt. I've been caring for my mom for the past fifteen years. I'm all she's got. I need some reinforcement here.

PASTOR. Sounds like you're feeling a real need for support. It must hurt to feel you're caring for your mom by yourself.

JANE. I know you're very busy. Do you think you could get by to see her this week?

PASTOR. Yes, indeed. I'm not sure what day it will be, but I'll be there. Thanks for letting me know how this is impacting you.

JANE. Thanks for being understanding, Pastor.

Part 2: Crisis Response

Notice in Example A that the pastor immediately defends himself. He completely ignores how Jane is feeling. He seems focused on the thought that people may be talking about him behind his back. His defensiveness only adds to the woman's chagrin, and she fights back with an accusation and a threat. The pastor plays the martyr card and grudgingly gives in to Jane's demand. The conversation drives a wedge between pastor and parishioner. This has been a lose-lose transaction.

In Example B, however, the pastor focuses entirely on Jane's feelings. He seeks not to defend himself or even apologize but to understand Jane. Perhaps it's unrealistic for Jane to expect her pastor to visit her mother, but the pastor doesn't bring that up. He doesn't seem the least bit worried about how he's perceived by the "lot of people" who might be concerned about his lack of care. Instead, the pastor wants to nurture the relationship in front of him. He listens calmly to Jane's concern, reflects her thoughts back to her, checks to make sure he's heard her correctly, and defuses her bitterness. Both parties leave the transaction with a new understanding of each other. Jane even got her way. Everyone wins.

Wouldn't it be great if every crisis in the church could be resolved by active listening? While that's expecting too much, I am confident that if we pastors were better listeners, many church hurricanes would come to a speedier end. I have learned through the years that people just want to know they have been heard. Once they know you've heard them, they will often back down. In fact, they might even become your biggest supporters. If urban violence could be curbed in Boston by a handful of ministers willing to listen to gang members, it is likely that ministry storms can be weakened if not eliminated by active listening.

When I look back on the storm that split New Life Church, I regret that I did not take time to listen to members of the church who were unhappy with the direction our worship ministry was taking. These were sincere followers of Jesus who found contemporary worship less than satisfying. Were they wrong? No. Their opinions about worship had been shaped over many years. It was insensitive of me to expect them to unquestioningly embrace the changes we had implemented. When I heard people reacting negatively to the addition of guitars and drums in worship, I retreated instead of going to them as a caring pastor. I should have met with the naysayers, listened to their concerns and fears, connected with them emotionally, and then—*then*—explained patiently and biblically why I thought the addition of contemporary elements in worship was good for the church and for our city. Why was I in such a hurry to change things? Why did I retreat instead of engaging people who disagreed with me? Could it be that I really did not love them? It hurts to say it, but a failure to listen is really a failure to love.

I realize that some church hurricanes are caused by important doctrinal differences and incompatible philosophies of ministry. Division is not always sinful, nor can all differences be resolved simply by listening to each other. We should celebrate the kaleidoscopic picture of the body of Christ displayed by the millions of churches and thousands of denominations around the world. My own denomination, the Presbyterian Church in America, emerged from theological conflict. I am not one to argue for unity that ignores substantive disagreements. Not until we are together on the new earth will the prayer of Jesus that we "become perfectly one" be at last fulfilled (John 17:23).

At the same time, many church storms flare up because human beings tend to view situations as either personal wins or losses. We see each other as either allies or enemies. Interpersonal conflict is as old as Genesis 3. As soon as Adam and Eve had eaten the forbidden fruit, they began pointing the finger of blame at each other. They hid behind fig leaves—weak attempts to ignore their shame and protect themselves from true relational intimacy. Sin ruined the original plan of God for humans to live together in holiness, harmony, and peace. Cain's murder of his brother Abel was

Part 2: Crisis Response

a sign that "desire when it has conceived gives birth to sin, and sin when it is fully grown brings forth death" (Jas 1:15).

Followers of Jesus are not immune to murderous, Cain-like impulses. We are, even as reborn individuals, *posse peccare*—able to sin. That is why churches, intended to be hospitals for the "weak and wounded, sick and sore," often become Antietam battlefields. Just yesterday I met a man who told me about the sinful conflict that has raged in his church for years. He said it began with a little thing. The pastor failed to visit someone in the hospital.

Now you know where I got the active listening example above.

Let's review the critical elements of a gospel-centered response to church conflict:

> **Summary of Part 2: Crisis Response**
>
> - Don't go it alone. Admit your weakness. Rely on a faithful band of brothers and sisters.
> - Speak truthfully, at all times and to all people—even the troublemakers.
> - Reach beyond your church to people with the skills to assist you.
> - Be willing not to engage or win every battle.
> - Pray often and hard. You have not because you ask not.
> - Be a good listener.

Part 3

Crisis Recovery

Chapter 13
Faith

IN PART 1 WE explored several ways to prepare for, if not avoid, a ministry-killing hurricane. In Part 2 we looked at six tactics for leading a church through storms into calmer weather. In this final section of *Surviving Ministry*, we turn our attention to recovery. I'm happy to say I recovered from the hurricane that pounded New Life Church. Or more accurately, I should say that I'm *in* recovery. It's turning out to be a long journey back to joy. Four things are contributing to my healing: faith, friends, family, and forgiveness. Let's start with *faith*.

Let us assume your ministry storm has passed but the jagged remains of harsh words, betrayal, disappointment, and failure lie scattered around the church, in your heart, and perhaps even in your own home. You are at some stage of burnout. You've lost that bright-eyed, boundless energy you had when you started out in ministry. How will you recover and move forward in life? Where do you go from here? Those are the questions that Darren is asking himself these days.

Darren is a steady, humble, compassionate man. He was a great pastor. A faithful teacher of God's Word. But one day, he crashed.

Part 3: Crisis Recovery

Fresh out of seminary three decades ago, Darren accepted a call to a small church in an Appalachian community. He was the first full-time pastor the church had ever had. The average age of its two dozen members was sixty-five. But Darren still carries warm memories of his time among them. He and his wife were married while he served in this little town. Their first child was born there. But it was clear Darren's gifts could be used in a wider sphere.

Darren moved his young family to a church in Alabama where he was the solo pastor for nearly ten years. They had a second child. The church held steady in membership. It was a happy experience. But a new opportunity presented itself in the spring of 2000. Darren accepted a call to a bigger church in another southern suburb.

This church, Darren told me, was dysfunctional. Darren's predecessor had been asked to leave. He had replaced a man who was highly regarded—not as a great preacher or administrative leader but as a warm, loving pastor. Unfortunately, Darren's predecessor was the very opposite. He just didn't fit. So when Darren arrived, he knew he would need to take his time, build trust, and give the church some much-needed stability. And he did just that.

Things went well for several years. Darren led a reorganization of the elder board and faithfully taught the Bible. But Darren found it a tough church to pastor. Theologically, people were all over the map. Some voiced their opposition to Darren's teaching. Others had bad attitudes toward church leaders. Members of the worship team wanted control. Previous elders had refused to confront sin in the church. Now, when the elders tried to put policies in place some members didn't like it. Disgruntled, a contingent left the church for greener grass. Several of Darren's key supporters and friends also left because of job changes. Worse yet, Darren's assistant pastor—a close friend—accepted a call to another church. These losses were hard on Darren and his wife.

Two other events pushed Darren over the edge. He had to put his beloved dog to sleep. But much more devastating, his mother was slowly declining into Alzheimer's disease. Darren knew she could no longer care for herself, so he moved her out of her house many miles away into an assisted living facility near him. She hated her new home. It was far away from everything familiar. She grew increasingly adversarial, begging Darren again and again to take her back home. But there was no way he could do that.

Darren's mom eventually passed in December, 2013. But her mental and emotional decline, on the heels of all the other losses Darren had experienced, took a terrible toll on him. He shut down emotionally and became almost nonfunctional. The day of the "crash," Darren's wife called the elders and said Darren would not be able to preach that weekend—and maybe not for a long while. He couldn't get out of bed. He could hardly even speak. For weeks, doing anything at all required enormous energy. Night after night he couldn't sleep. He says he was never suicidal, but he felt overcome with stress, sadness, and fear.

A caring, older couple invited Darren and his wife to move into their home for as long as they needed. Darren took the next two months off. He got counseling and started taking an antidepressant. Slowly the darkness began to lift. He eventually felt like doing a bit of church work. The congregation was very understanding, he says. He was honest with them. He told them about his stress, his sadness, his tendency to isolate himself and not depend on the help of others. Being vulnerable and open actually drew him closer to his people. He grew more understanding of people's pain. He says, "I learned the value of sighing."

But in the months following his return, Darren realized something had changed inside him. He no longer felt that he fit as a senior or solo pastor. So Darren resigned.

Darren is now asking the questions he says he should have asked a long time ago: "What's my gift mix? Where does God want me? What was I made for?" Darren is considering teaching, writing, and mentoring younger pastors. "I'm ready for something different now," he says.

Darren is actually a friend of mine. He and I were in seminary together. We'd lost track of each other over the years but, oddly enough, we got back together through Twitter. I was at a conference in Houston a couple years ago with more than a thousand pastors. As I looked around at all those men and women in ministry I thought to myself, "Wonder how many of these pastors are depressed, hurting, or lonely?" On a whim I put that rhetorical question into a tweet, hashtagged the conference, and sent it out. In no time at all, I picked up a number of new Twitter followers. Six people favorited my tweet. Several friends at the conference who had seen my tweet came up and thanked me for it. I'm guessing they just needed someone to tell them they weren't crazy. One of them was my friend Darren.

From our time in seminary I remembered Darren as a brilliant, humble fellow. But here he was thirty years later, sighing and wondering what to do next. I asked Darren what, if anything, might have prevented him from crashing in ministry. He told me, "If I had just grasped that God is for me; that would have helped."

When I talk to pastors, I can tell many of them are where Darren was. They don't really grasp that God is *for them*. And for the longest time, I didn't either. I told you in chapter 4 that one spring day in 1975 I came to the end of myself and ran to Jesus. I embraced the One who had embraced me on the cross. "He took my heart for his own home, and let me know I'm not alone," as Billy Crockett sang. But then time passed, I became a pastor, and some of the old insecurities returned. I never doubted my salvation, but I did question God's love for me. How could God love a guy who didn't always love him back? How could God be for a guy who kept on sinning the same sins, who hurt people sometimes and did such a poor job of being holy and pure? To quiet my conscience, I strove to excel at preaching and leading my church. Every sermon had to be perfect and make a lasting impression on the congregation. When my sermon got a lot of pats on the back I had a great week, but when it fell flat I hated myself for days. I fed off compliments and was crushed by criticism. I was building a reputation, so I couldn't admit weakness. I couldn't make a mistake. I had to be the best pastor, the best preacher, the best leader my congregation had ever had. I wanted them to talk about me in glowing terms and tell their friends what a great minister I was.

In a very real sense, being a pastor had become a self-salvation project, a way to avoid God and use people. Like Harold Abrahams in the movie *Chariots of Fire* who said every footrace was a means of justifying his existence, I looked at every talk, every meeting, every pastoral visit as a means of self-justification. Henri Nouwen once said in a sermon, "As long as we continue to live as if we are what we do, what we have, and what other people think about us, we will remain filled with judgments, opinions, evaluations, and condemnations. We will remain addicted to putting people and things in their 'right' place."[1] And yes, that's exactly what I was doing.

In the early 1990s, thanks to World Harvest Mission's *Sonship* course, the sunshine of the gospel broke through the clouds and I understood, perhaps for the first time, that God really is for me. I saw him no longer as my Boss but my loving Father. I realized that the more I sought to build my own record, the less I was living by faith in the perfect record of Jesus Christ. Faith means trusting not in our works but in the work Jesus did on our behalf. No matter how badly we've screwed up, where we've been, what we've done, or whom we've done it to, God's love for us is sure because it's rooted in Jesus. Like Paul said to his Colossian friends, "And you, who once were alienated and hostile in mind, doing evil deeds, [Jesus] has now reconciled in his body of flesh by his death, in order to present you holy and blameless and above reproach before [the Father]" (Col 1:21–22).

All our mistakes, all our failures, all our bad decisions, all our unloving thoughts, words, and deeds are covered by the blood of Christ. He lived the life we should have lived and died the death we deserve to die. Faith means trusting that what Jesus did through his active and passive obedience for us is sufficient. We stand in Christ complete and free of accusation. As Paul continues in Colossians, "And you, who were dead in your trespasses and the

---

1. Nouwen, *Here and Now*, 81.

uncircumcision of your flesh, God made alive together with [Jesus], having forgiven us all our trespasses, by canceling the record of debt that stood against us with its legal demands. This he set aside, nailing it to the cross" (Col 2:13–14).

People may condemn us, but God does not. In fact, as the prophet Zephaniah reminds us, God is right now rejoicing over us with gladness and exulting over us with loud singing (Zeph 3:17). This is because, through faith and repentance, we have been once for all united with Christ in his death, burial, resurrection, and ascension. This is the gospel: "For our sake [God] made [Jesus] to be sin who knew no sin, so that in [Jesus] we might become the righteousness of God" (2 Cor 5:21). The glorious exchange that took place on the cross 2,000 years ago—our sins transferred to Jesus, his righteousness transferred to us—means that nothing we do could possibly make God love us more, and nothing we do could possibly cause God to love us less.

I played football in high school. Though I was small, I was a pretty mean linebacker. But there was one game when I was completely out of energy. It was the fourth quarter and I was so tired there was no way I could go back out on the field when the other team took over on offense. But I didn't want to tell Coach. So I came up with a clever plan. A kid named Ricky was my back up. When Coach was not looking, I pulled Ricky over on the sidelines and asked him to take my place on defense. I told him, "Let's exchange jerseys and the coach will never know the difference." So we took off our jerseys. I put on his jersey and he put on mine and went out on the field to play my position. Now Ricky was wearing my number, and I was wearing his. Wouldn't you know it? He caught an interception. Over the loudspeaker the game announcer said, "Mike Osborne with the interception!" I got the glory; Ricky did the work.

By sending Ricky out on the field I trusted him to do what I couldn't do for myself. In just the same way, Christians are people who know they are so sinful they cannot possibly save themselves. They are trusting that Jesus paid it all. Through repentance and faith, they get the glory of peace with God, sins forgiven, the indwelling Holy Spirit, the promise of eternal life—and Jesus gladly does all the work.

What are the practical implications of this good news for us church leaders? Two things come to mind. One is that we should never seek our identity in ministry success or failure. We are defined neither by our wins nor by our losses, neither by the number of people who adore us nor by the number of people who can't stand us. Rather, our identity is rooted in Jesus' performance for us, which is constant and perfect. Faith in Jesus frees us to be neither crushed by failure nor puffed up by success. Faith in Jesus creates genuine gospel humility. Jesus loves us because he loves us.

The other implication is that weakness is our greatest asset. The way up is down. To admit brokenness is actually the way to open our hearts—and our churches—to God's grace and power. We know that Paul struggled mightily with some kind of besetting sin or weakness that he called a thorn in his flesh. Many scholars suggest it was a physical disability. Could it have been recurring depression? The loneliness of being single? A stubborn sin like lust or envy? Perhaps. Whatever the case, despite his prayers to be free of that thorn, God said no and told Paul, "My grace is sufficient for you, for my power is made perfect in weakness" (2 Cor 12:9). Paul was able to boast shamelessly about his weaknesses, because he knew the secret: Grace flows downhill. The deeper we go in honest admission of sin and failure, the stronger we become in the grace of God.

Martin Luther famously said, "The truth of the gospel is the principle article of all Christian doctrine . . . Most necessary is it that we know this article well, teach it to others, and beat it into their heads continually."[2] Perhaps you've never doubted God's love like Darren or me or billions of other Christians, and this chapter has been a restatement of the obvious. But most pastors I know need

---

2. Luther, *A Commentary on St. Paul's Epistle to the Galatians*, p. 101.

the gospel beaten into their heads again and again. We need to preach it as often to ourselves as to our congregations. "For in [the gospel] the righteousness of God is revealed from faith for faith" (Rom 1:17). That is the Bible verse that set Martin Luther free.

It set me free. It can set you free as well.

Chapter 14
Friends

BEN AND HIS WIFE Marlene were Baptist missionaries in Mali, West Africa. Getting there had not been easy. Months of training in the States had been interrupted when one of their three children was diagnosed with an anxiety disorder known as selective mutism. She had to have several months of counseling. Then, just when they thought everything was taken care of, their supervisors in Mali were sent back to the United States to recover from burnout. Ben, Marlene, and the kids had to live in Senegal for two months, where they didn't speak the language and felt all alone.

Now in Mali, the couple immersed themselves in French and Bambara language training. Their kids went to a school for missionary children. For a while, the family loved being in Mali. Not only were there plenty of people with whom to share the gospel; they also met friendly missionaries whose homes were always open to each other. "We would throw mattresses on the floor and have sleepovers for each other's kids," Ben says.

But as time went on, Ben realized that "friendly" does not equal "friends." There was a kind of competitiveness among the missionaries. Instead of someone asking, "How are you doing?" the questions were always, "How many villages have you visited? How many people have you shared Christ with?" Mission work seemed to be all about results. Ben and Marlene missed their church back home where pastors and friends formed a support system. Here in Mali that system was missing. There was support for the physical difficulties of living in Mali where, for example, the power would often go off for an entire day. But Ben and Marlene felt alone spiritually and emotionally. They had no one to help address the spiritual impact of living in a third-world country without church community. Sundays offered no respite; that was the day all the missionaries scattered to the villages for Bible storytelling. Ben says he and Marlene learned to suffer in silence. He coped with the lack of community by simply persevering. "That's what I felt I had to do: give, give, give, never receive. I wasn't happy, but I had to keep going for Jesus." In time, Ben concluded the more miserable and lonely he was, the more he must be doing the work of the Lord.

When war erupted in Mali in 2012, the family had to relocate to Berkina Faso. Ben became an emotional mess. He would cry easily, get angry and depressed, and fight with Marlene. Marlene didn't understand what was happening to Ben; he didn't understand it himself. All he knew is that he felt very alone.

A death in Marlene's family sent the family back to the United States. They ended up staying for almost a year. They thought things would improve between them, but they did not. Ben and Marlene could have reached out and asked for help; they could have gone to counseling. But they were too embarrassed.

Continuing turmoil in Mali led the mission board to send the family to Botswana. "As soon as we stepped off the plane, we knew we didn't belong there," Marlene says. "We hated it from day one." Arguments between Ben and her escalated. Ben continued to feel depressed, lonely, and angry. They stuck it out for two years in Botswana. But at last they raised the white flag. "We need help," Ben said. They went to South Africa for an intensive month of counseling and then returned to the States for good.

Although things are better now for Ben and Marlene, they are still fragile. Through counseling, Ben is discovering the identity issues that lay behind his anger and depression. Marlene has found a full-time job and Ben is considering a youth pastor position. Ben looks back on their years in Africa with gratitude: "I never would

FRIENDS

have learned these lessons any other way. It was painful but I'm glad I went through it. I'm a work in progress. I'm learning a new way to live, a new way to view myself. I am someone God is redeeming, not just using."

He's also learned the value of community. "The church needs to be a place where you don't have to put on a happy face and act like everything's fine when it's not. Things are going to happen in ministry. You need a place to go where you can suffer out loud."

Unfortunately, Ben and Marlene's experience on the mission field is similar to that of many pastors in the United States. "Friendly" does not always equal "friends" in the American church. According to researchers, approximately seventy percent of pastors say they have no close friends.[1] A 2009 Lilly Endowment study of three Christian denominations found that most pastors lack strong friendships with other pastors.[2] I've lost count of the number of ministers who have told me they are lonely. They have many acquaintances and colleagues—but friends? Not so much. Most of our social interactions are about what we call "ministry." When we are with people we are in charge and on the clock. They are looking to us for leadership, direction, or support, not friendship. When we meet with someone it is usually because we are helping solve a problem, telling someone what to do, collaborating on an event, or explaining Christian truth, not enjoying one another.

Besides, pastors are like all human beings: we fear intimacy. We will find excuses not to pursue community. In his bestselling book, *Bowling Alone*, Professor Robert Putnam charts the recent rise of isolation in America. Everyone seems to be withdrawing from social intercourse, he says. "We know our neighbors less well,

---

1. Wilson, Michael T. and Brad Hoffmann, *Preventing Ministry Failure*. Downers Grove, IL: IVP Books, 2007, p. 31, quoted in J. R. Briggs, *Fail: Finding Hope and Grace in the Midst of Ministry Failure*. Downers Grove, IL: IVP Books, 2014, p. 47.

2. Bloom, "Well-Lived Pastoral Life: Summary of Results from the Initial Survey."

and we see old friends less often."³ But pastors are particularly at risk when it comes to loneliness. Studying the Bible, coming up with a constant stream of creative sermons and talks, and maintaining a quality devotional life require many hours of isolation. While most adults can put a cap on the number of people in their social circle, pastors must be friendly all the time to everybody. As Pastor Mark Brouwer writes, "We have too many relationships and too few friends."⁴

Furthermore, choosing people with whom to build a friendship is always a risky venture, but especially for pastors. Church members can be jealous when they perceive they are not in their pastor's inner circle. This was an issue at a church I once served as associate pastor. Several congregation members confided in me that they felt second-class because they weren't in the senior pastor's cadre of favorite people. Pastors occupy dual roles with those they call friends. They are both "over" them as their spiritual leader and "beside" them as their friend—a difficult tension to maintain. "No matter how hard a leader wishes to be a regular person, it is just not possible," writes Dan Allender.⁵ Brouwer continues,

> Often pastors will identify people in their church as friends who are also church board members. These board members often have the task of deciding on compensation for, and sometimes the discipline and termination of, the pastor. Can we have a completely transparent, reciprocal relationship with someone who looks to us as their spiritual teacher and leader or who serves in the role of corporate supervisor? It's highly unlikely.⁶

What is a friend? A friend is someone who knows us and loves us anyway. A friend is someone with whom we can let down our guard, say exactly what we're thinking, and not be rejected. A pastor I know says that a friend is someone who will listen to our

3. Putnam, *Bowling Alone*, 115.
4. Brouwer, "Friendless Pastor," lines 4–5.
5. Allender, *Leading with a Limp*, 109.
6. Brouwer, "Friendless Pastor," lines 78–84.

hurts and still call us Christian. Further, a friend is someone with whom we feel perfectly safe yet who still calls us to Christlikeness. Tim Keller, noted pastor of Redeemer Presbyterian Church in Manhattan, says, "Friendship is a deep oneness that develops as two people, speaking the truth in love to each other, journey together to the same horizon."[7] By these definitions, we are extremely blessed if we have more than a handful of friends over a lifetime. According to the writer of Proverbs, "A man of many companions may come to ruin, but there is a friend who sticks closer than a brother" (Prov 18:24). While we might be tempted to read Christ into that Bible verse, I doubt Solomon was thinking about the Messiah. Instead, he was describing what wise men and women do: they choose to cultivate one or two friendships that are closer than family.

I admit that pursuing friendship with people in the church is fraught with risk and uncertainty. But I will argue that it's worth the gamble. We who lead the church need the church. Paul David Tripp writes, "[I]f Christ is the head of his body, then everything else is just body, including the pastor, and therefore the pastor needs what the body has been designed to deliver."[8] And let me add that those of us who are married need a friend who is not our spouse. A key element in my recovery from the crisis that was New Life Church was having a handful of friends with whom to walk through the fire, of whom most were men. They were members of my church. My wife and I were in a small group consisting of six other people. That small group was our lifeline. Both during the turmoil and after things died down, this group held us up in prayer, listened to our pain, cried with us, made us laugh, did not condemn us, and helped us figure out what to do next. I would not have experienced renewed joy in ministry without these friends. They were the kiss of God to me. In my current pastorate I have two friends in the church with whom I meet regularly for confession, affirmation, and encouragement. I meet at least monthly with

---

7. Keller, *The Meaning of Marriage: Facing the Complexities of Commitment with the Wisdom of God*, 127.

8. Tripp, *Dangerous Calling*, 88.

a pastor in a nearby community; he and I have been friends since our seminary days when we lived in neighboring apartments. How kind of God to bring us back together in the same city. I also have a good friend who lives 100 miles away. We text or email each other almost every day for encouragement and accountability.

I worry about pastors who choose not to pursue friendship. Allender says, "A leader with no close friends is a leader who is prone to swing between hiding and manipulating."[9] Without a friend one must find unhealthy ways of coping with the pain of living. Sinful habits and toxic attitudes grow in the soil of isolation.

Jesus came into our world to do more than reconcile us to God, as glorious as that is. He also came to reconcile us to each other. The gospel is what makes friendship among sinners possible. Think about David and Jonathan's friendship. Here were two young men from vastly different worlds. One grew up herding sheep in obscurity; the other ate from a silver spoon surrounded by the privileges of royalty. After David killed Goliath of Gath, King Saul grew insanely jealous of David. You would expect Jonathan, son of Saul, to have reacted the same way. After all, Jonathan was the presumed heir to the throne of Israel. But instead of envying David for his increasing popularity, "the soul of Jonathan was knit to the soul of David, and Jonathan loved him as his own soul" (1 Sam 18:1). This is Scripture's way of describing deep friendship. The passage goes on to say, "Then Jonathan made a covenant with David, because he loved him as his own soul. And Jonathan stripped himself of the robe that was on him and gave it to David, and his armor, and even his sword and his bow and his belt" (1 Sam 18:3-4). As many readers will know, the making or "cutting" of a covenant in the Bible is a promise of loyalty to the death. A covenant is a solemn bond in blood requiring the death of the covenant breaker. For Jonathan to remove his robe and give it to David was an act of faith in David's future calling to be king. His gifts of armor, sword, bow, and belt—precious items in those days—amounted to a relinquishing

---

9. Allender, *Leading with a Limp*, 114.

of his right to the throne and a symbolic giving of his entire self to David. Later, as Saul's hatred of David grew, Jonathan protected David and literally risked his life for him. Because of the covenant, Jonathan had David's back.

More than just an inspiring picture of human friendship, the story of Jonathan's love for David points to Jesus, who set aside the privileges of deity on the cross and gave his entire self to us in inviolable covenant love. "[T]hough he was in the form of God, [he] did not count equality with God a thing to be grasped, but emptied himself, by taking the form of a servant, being born in the likeness of men. And being found in human form, he humbled himself by becoming obedient to the point of death, even death on a cross" (Phil 2:6–8).

Because of the cross, Jesus no longer calls us servants but friends. Speaking of his imminent death Jesus said, "Greater love has no one than this, that someone lay down his life for his friends" (John 15:13–15). Jesus made sinners his friends so that sinners can make friends of fellow sinners. Friendship with God sets us free from the shame and fear caused by sin and gives us the courage we need to pursue deep covenant friendship with other people.

So how might ministers of the gospel develop friendships even as they lead God's people? Here are six lessons I have learned:

Be Careful

This might seem strange advice given all I've said about friendship. But there are people in the body of Christ who will turn on you, betray you, and use your own words to bring you down. Do not let down your guard to just anyone, especially when you are new in a church. Friendship implies deep trust and vulnerability. You will be wise to get to know people for a year or so before you unveil your heart to someone. Be an observer during that year. Build relationships but be careful with your heart. The writer of Proverbs warns, "Make no friendship with a man given to anger, nor go with a wrathful man, lest you learn his ways and entangle yourself in a snare" (Prov 22:24–25). Even Jesus "did not entrust himself to [people], because he knew all people and needed no one to bear witness about man, for he himself knew what was in man" (John 2:24–25). I write from experience. One of the mistakes I made at New Life Church was prematurely opening up too much to people. I misjudged key people who seemed friendly at first but made life miserable for me later. Take your time and allow the Lord to knit your heart together with a few people—in his own time.

Be Intentional

You cannot pursue friendship without making it a priority. Friends create pockets of time for friends. Friends budget money for babysitters and hospitality and dining out with friends. Don't let ministry duties crowd out friendship. Making and maintaining friendship doesn't happen automatically. Obviously emergencies will arise. But don't sacrifice friendship on the altar of ministry. Having good friends will actually make you a better pastor.

Be Honest

To be a friend, we have to come out of hiding. We must be willing to risk rejection and let our friends know where we are. Marc is one of my friends at the church I currently serve. Marc has a unique way of asking me how I'm doing. Instead of the usual "How are you?" Marc asks, "Where is your red dot?" At first I didn't know what to make of that. "What's the 'red dot'?" I asked. He explained that in the lobbies of most shopping malls there is a big map in a display case. On that map there is usually a big red dot or arrow that says, "You are here." So when Marc asks me where's my red dot, what he means is, "Where are you, Mike?" He's asking me the same question God asked Adam after Adam had eaten the forbidden fruit: "Where are you, Adam (Gen 3:9)? Where's your red dot?" God was inviting Adam to come out of hiding and be honest about his sin. That's what friends do for each other. Let your friend know where you are.

Be Committed

I've always been blown away by the four friends in Mark 2 who took their paralyzed friend to Jesus (Mark 2:1–12). They let nothing stand in the way—not busyness, cynicism, embarrassment, fatigue, or even a rooftop. With a little Yiddish ingenuity, the four friends figured out how to rig up a litter, remove a few roof tiles, and lower the paralytic down to Jesus. That was a risky maneuver. Who knew what the owner of the house might do to these four EMT wannabes? No telling how much those roof repairs were going to cost them. No matter. They were committed to their friend's healing.

Be There

Solomon said, "A friend loves at all times, and a brother is born for adversity" (Prov 17:17). One of my great regrets in life is that I've failed to show up for friends at a few key moments. Several years ago a mentor of mine died of cancer. His funeral was held in the Midwest, many miles away from where I was living, and I did not go. I wish I had. This was a man who helped shaped me into the man I am today. I should have been there to hug his wife and thank her, but I didn't go. Since then I've resolved to do everything in my power to be there when a friend of mine is hurting, no matter the cost. Physical presence is one of the most powerful of all acts of friendship.

Be Creative

If it's not safe or possible to develop a few deep friendships in your church, look elsewhere. Ask God to surprise you with an unlikely Jonathan. Pursue the pastor of a nearby church, a neighbor,

PART 3: CRISIS RECOVERY

someone you often see at the gym or coffee shop, or an old friend with whom you've lost touch. Join a book club, a bike club, a tennis league. I once met a man at one of my son's T-ball games. We struck up a conversation, started hanging out together, and eventually he became my best friend.

Whatever you do, don't be a friendless pastor.

Chapter 15
Family

NEWS FLASH: AMERICAN FAMILIES are under assault.

While that is no surprise, it shocks many churchgoers to learn that the families of pastors are under assault too. Thom Rainer, president and CEO of LifeWay Christian Resources, writes, "If I were to devise a scheme to destroy churches, I would find ways to attack the pastor. And as I found ways to attack the pastor, I would see his family as the area of greatest vulnerability. Attack the church by attacking the pastor. Attack the pastor by attacking his family."[1]

Widely quoted statistics indicate that most pastors feel that being in ministry negatively affects their family.[2] While some recent research suggests that number has been overblown,[3] there is no doubt that all is not well in the homes of many church leaders. Many pastors feel under pressure to have a model family, while underneath the veneer are wounds of loneliness, resentment, and rage that never heal. And when the church is in crisis, family relationships take an especially hard hit. It is my contention in this chapter that recovery from church hurricanes must be a family

---

1. Rainer, "Seven Ways the Pastor's Family Comes under Attack," lines 1–4.

2. Sherman, "Pastor Burnout Statistics," lines 26–67.

3. Stetzer, "That Stat That Says Pastors Are All Miserable and Want to Quit (Part 1)," lines 8–104.

affair. Spouse and children suffer the effects of church strife along with us, and we must journey toward recovery together. Like faith and friends, our family can be a powerful agent of restoration. But we have to understand what our loved ones have experienced and what they may have lost during the storm.

I have referred to my five difficult years at New Life Church throughout this book. As the storms of controversy and strife intensified, I grew more and more despondent and detached from my wife Suzy. She in turn felt abandoned by me and angry at those who were causing me pain. In her own words, "I was angry that people would treat my husband and family the way they did. Did they think the conflicts at church would not affect me and our children? What happened to grace and love? But as a pastor's wife I couldn't really do anything about it." When our church split over worship style differences, most of our friends chose to go to the new "contemporary" church. To my wife it was "like a dagger in the heart." After that, Suzy stayed home many Sundays instead of going to church. During the week she had graduate school to keep her preoccupied, but she spent weekends crying.

Suzy felt she was in a helpless position. Except for her counselor and one or two friends, my wife had nowhere safe to unload her distress. Nor did she have any authority to be able to change things. Neither of us could tell our friends what was really going on behind the scenes. The gulf between Suzy and me widened. I was spending more and more of my time at elder board meetings that often went past 11:00 p.m. and coming home crushed in spirit. My wife was attending nursing school, dealing with two challenging teenagers, and adjusting to life without our daughter who was now a college student 600 miles away. Finances were tight; our house was a money pit. Suzy has often remarked that the drought in our part of the country during those five years was a metaphor for how dry we felt emotionally, spiritually, and relationally. There were some happy times, but we fought a lot and cried a lot.

FAMILY

Suzy notes that when things go down in a church, the pastor is affected in ways someone in a different field might not be. An unhappy employee can give a two-week notice and look for a job in another company. But we pastors have to uproot our family and move to a new city. Our mistakes are public, the subject of coffee shop conversations and email chains. Friendships are disrupted, ties severed. Children must start over with new teachers, new schools, a new neighborhood.

I asked my children (now adults in their twenties and thirties) to share their perspectives on our five troubled New Life years. Here's what my youngest son had to say:

> I didn't know what was going on until you had already decided that we needed to move. It was confusing and frustrating for me. I knew about all the strife the church was going through, but not how it was causing you and Mom personal pain. Sure, there were nights where you seemed kind of tired and defeated, and Mom was crying in the kitchen, but even people with happy childhoods understand that's what life is like occasionally. To me at the time, it seemed like everything was fine with us and then, all of a sudden, you were saying I had to leave all my friends and what I knew behind.

Earlier in this book, I referenced Jonathan Edwards's farewell sermon preached to his Northampton congregation in 1750. In that sermon he said,

> We have had great disputes how the church ought to be regulated, and indeed the subject of these disputes was of great importance; but the due regulation of your families is of no less, and in some respects of much greater, importance. *Every Christian family ought to be as it were a little church,* consecrated to Christ, and wholly influenced and governed by His rules. And family education and order are some of the chief of the means of grace. If these fail, all other means are likely to prove ineffectual.

Part 3: Crisis Recovery

If these are duly maintained, all the means of grace will be likely to prosper and be successful.[4] (emphasis mine)

Now there's a great line: "Every Christian family ought to be a little church." But what a challenge for us pastors. We have *two* churches to care for—our "big church" and our "little church." How can we be faithful shepherds of them both, especially when we're picking up the pieces of conflict in the big church? Here are four lessons I've learned that can help families recover from ministry trauma.

Live Transparently in Your Home

While I stayed involved in my children's lives during our years at New Life Church, I was not fully honest with them about the storms swirling around me. I judged it best not to talk about the things and people making my life miserable. When people betray us, when fellow leaders sabotage our ministry, when church members criticize and spread false rumors about us, it's hard to speak in glowing terms about the church and its people. If we talk about our adversaries negatively we risk planting seeds of bitterness in our children's hearts. The fact that we are hurting and confused does not justify the sin of gossip. We want our children to develop a love for the Lord and the local church even when we are going through the junk of ministry.

But in retrospect, I should have been more transparent. Children have an uncanny aptitude for reading the lines of anguish on our face even when we don't say anything. My kids knew something was wrong, but because their worlds were relatively stable they didn't fully understand what it was.

My older son, now age thirty-four, shared this insight:

> A pastor should share stories with his kids about what he's dealing with (where privacy isn't an issue), his pastoral philosophy, his feelings about whether he's doing a good job handling it, etc. Allowing your kids to experience

---

4. Edwards, "Farewell Sermon," 27.

FAMILY

your ministry along with you helps them see the good things that church leaders do and understand how often we fail in trying to do God's work. It's more likely that the kids will see themselves in competition with work for their dad's attention if you don't talk about why you're at a late meeting or have to leave the house on Saturdays.

I have decided it would have been good to level with my children about what I was going through at New Life—as long as I did not slander the slanderers and criticize the critics. Being honest but loving would have given me an opportunity to model the teaching of Jesus: "Love your enemies, do good to those who hate you, bless those who curse you, pray for those who abuse you . . . And as you wish that others would do to you, do so to them" (Luke 6:27–31). The struggles the church was going through could have become matter for family prayer and scripture reading. Who knows? My children might have had wise words of advice for this stressed-out pastor.

Don't Stop Being a Family

Just because winds of strife are pounding the church does not mean we throw the family overboard. A pastor friend who knew I was writing this book emailed me this bit of well-known but oft-forgotten wisdom: "First Jesus, then your family, then the ministry. Whenever the order gets out of place, that's when trouble starts." Authors H. B. London, Jr., and Neil Wiseman offer similar advice: "Please the people who matter most."[5]

If only it were so simple, right? As every pastor knows, ministry often interrupts family life. How many times have you had to cut short your vacation to fly home to the bedside of a dying parishioner and prepare a funeral message? The fact that I'm writing this book while on sabbatical did not exempt me from dealing with a suicide threat in my congregation just this morning. Pastors who are spouses and/or parents face the daily tension

---

5. London and Wiseman, *Pastors at Greater Risk*, 167.

between faithfulness at church and faithfulness at home. This tension is heightened when churches are in a season of strife or controversy. During such seasons we may not have the liberty to say no to members who need to talk, to walk out while a meeting is in progress, or finish our dinner date with our spouse. The call to ministry is a call to the whole family to sacrifice time together when gospel priorities require it. Some pastors turn their spouse or children into an idol that they dare not inconvenience. In those cases, "family first" becomes a poor excuse for going AWOL.

Having said that, however, I wonder what is really motivating us when we allow the needs of our church to trump the needs of our family. Is it really our selfless desire to serve Jesus and love our congregation? Or could it be that we need to be needed? Another pastor I know pointed out, "Maybe we spend all those hours at the church because that is where our egos get stroked. We are building *our* kingdom at the expense of our families where things are often messier and our contribution not easily measured." In their book, *The Pastor's Family*, Brian and Cara Croft write, "A pastor's heart is no different from any other heart (in desiring significance, or success). A pastor's neglect of his family cannot simply be blamed on the pressures, demands, and unrealistic expectations that have been placed on him. In the end, the struggle he faces—and the neglect of the family—has one root cause: a sinful heart."[6]

The fact is, our family is our first church. If things are crumbling at home, we will be in no shape to lead our church into brighter weather. That is why the Bible says elders must be good household managers, "for if someone does not know how to manage his own household, how will he care for God's church?" (1 Tim 3:5). If we must succeed somewhere, let us strive to succeed at home. Just as there will always be the poor among us (Matt 26:11), so the church will always have problems. There will be another controversy to settle, another battle to fight, another division to mend. Time will heal many ministry wounds. But time with your children has an expiration date. One pastor gave me this valuable rule of thumb: "Make decisions based on what is best for your family, not on what

---

6. Croft and Croft, *Pastor's Family*, 45.

might look good to the church or what criticism you think might come from the church."

Hand the church over to God and focus on your family. It's his church anyway, not yours. Have fun with your family, even if the church is coming apart. Maintain a regular date night with your spouse and don't violate it. Pull out Monopoly or Scrabble or Jenga or Cranium or Candy Land and play it with your kids. Go out for ice cream. Take your children fishing. Go on vacations. Use all your vacation time. Leave the tension in your office and please the people who matter the most.

Release Your Family from Misguided Expectations

I have a friend who writes a blog. She calls it *Not All Together*. I love that title because it honestly describes every human being who has ever lived but one: Jesus. Pastors and pastors' families are not all together. But congregations think we are, or at least expect us to be. They get this idea from reading idealized biographies of missionaries and Christian leaders, watching "Christian television," and hearing stories from pastors themselves about their wonderful marriage and family life. Plus, it's a foregone conclusion in their minds that anyone who spends so much time studying the Bible, praying, and leading people to Jesus must have a home life beyond compare.

My wife and I have not had the ideal marriage. Far from it. We've fought, struggled to communicate, failed to understand each other, slept in different rooms a few times, and gotten lots of marriage counseling. Nor have I been the perfect father. I didn't talk to my children enough. I was often preoccupied at home. I could have done much more to prepare them for adulthood. And to be honest, my kids were not the perfect kids. I won't embarrass them by writing about them here, but take my word for it: They've made their share of mistakes.

The pastors I hang out with admit to similar imperfections. But two-thirds of pastors' families say they feel pressure to be the

Part 3: Crisis Recovery

"ideal family."[7] One PK (pastor's kid) describes his childhood this way:

> PKs live in a fishbowl, or at least it feels that way. Everyone in the church knows the names and faces of the pastor's children. There is never the safety of anonymity. Details of our lives are known by people we recognize only from the church directory. Big church or small church, the same holds true. And while this isn't inherently harmful or problematic, the fact remains that fishbowls are for fish, not people. It is mighty hard to live a life surrounded by people knowing your every move, romantic interest, misbehavior, athletic triumph (or failure), college choice, and seemingly every other personal detail. This fishbowl experience magnifies the already elephantine expectations that PKs feel. With people watching every move, what room is there for a mistake? There can be no missteps, no dalliances, no failings. In short, there can be no humanity. See, PKs are no different than anyone else. We sin. We fail. But there is no being normal when everyone is watching.[8]

I asked my oldest child, now a pastor's wife and mother of three, to comment on what church leaders can do about the fishbowl phenomenon. Here's what she had to say:

> The truth about us is we are sinners on the inside. Trying to cover it up by looking nice or all together on the outside is just ridiculous. Obviously pastors' families are put on a pedestal. It's the pastor's job to fight against that for his family so they are free to be who they really are. An authentic pastor's family sets the tone for the rest of the church: "Here I am; please be who you are." I want my kids to be who they are, faults and all, because that's who God loves. It's up to us as parents not to burden our kids with standing stiffly on a pedestal but to give them the freedom to move around within God's grace.

---

7. Ibid., 148.
8. Piper, "Sinners in a Fishbowl," lines 18–30.

FAMILY

To these suggestions I would add the following: Be real in the pulpit; let your congregation know your mistakes as a spouse and parent. Don't perpetuate the myth of the perfect pastor's family. Emphasize to your children they don't have to be a certain kind of kid simply because you're a pastor. Delight in their unique personality traits. Never say to them, "People are watching you, you know." Let them follow their dreams and pursue their passions. And the same goes for your spouse: He or she does not have to occupy the stereotypical role of choir director or Bible study teacher or elder. Your spouse is a member of the church—that's all. Your spouse has spiritual gifts and interests and loves that need to be explored, just like everyone else. Affirm your spouse's individuality and protect him or her from unbiblical expectations.

Speak Positively about the Church

My elder daughter went on to say,

> We have tried with our kids to keep them aware of the blessings of being in ministry. We will tell them, "Sometimes Daddy has to miss something special or we might have to give something up, but we get other things in return." Pastors' families get a unique glimpse into God's kingdom at work. They get to see and hear about lives being changed. My hope is that this helps anytime my children feel they're missing out because of their dad's weird schedule and involvement with people. I want them to know the joy of being in ministry so that in the end, whether they end up in ministry or not, they will have a love for God's people.

Even if we've been hurt by the church, it's still the Bride of Christ. Singer-songwriter Sheila Walsh affirms this truth in her song *Jesus Loves the Church*.

> We fight like selfish children vying for that special prize
> We struggle with our gifts, before your face
> And I know you look with sorrow at the blindness in our eyes

Part 3: Crisis Recovery

> As we trip each other halfway through the race
> For we crucify each other leaving a battered wounded bride,
> But Jesus loves the church
> So we'll walk the aisle of history towards the marriage feast
> For Jesus loves the church[9]

Walsh is right: the church is a battered, wounded piece of work, but she is Jesus' beloved Bride all the same. As Rob Bentz writes in *The Unfinished Church*, "We're quirky, messy, and stained by sin," but we're still *his* church.[10] The church shoots its wounded sometimes, but she's still "a holy temple in the Lord" (Eph 2:21). And remember: to be a pastor is an incredible gift from God. We get to study, teach, and preach God's Word with tools and knowledge most Christians don't have. Every day we get to handle "things into which angels long to look" (1 Pet 1:12). It's our privilege to labor as though giving birth "until Christ is formed" in our congregation (Gal 4:19). We get to walk with God's people from cradle to grave, through all the key peaks and valleys of life. We get to baptize covenant children and converted adults, to welcome Spirit-born people into the family of God, to unite couples in holy matrimony, to whisper the final words and sing the final hymns people hear before they enter the joy of their Lord. We are "ambassadors of Christ" to whom God has committed "the ministry of reconciliation" (2 Cor 5:16–21). Can there be a more exciting, honored vocation?

But of course we easily lose sight of these privileges. During my difficult years at New Life Church, I grew depressed, anxious, and angry. I considered leaving the ministry. But with time came a break in the clouds, and I once again saw that we who are pastors are people with a dangerous but high calling.

Our children's view of the church (and of God) is shaped largely by how we feel about our work. If we drag ourselves out the door and complain about "having" to visit someone in the

---

9. "Jesus Loves the Church," by Sheila Walsh/Dave Cooke. ©1998 Word Music, LLC, Cooke Patch Music. All Rights Reserved. Used by Permission.

10. Bentz, *Unfinished Church*, 72.

FAMILY

hospital, attend an elders' meeting, or prepare a sermon, our children will likely talk about "having" to pray or give money or go to church someday. If we criticize our fellow leaders and gossip about those disrupting the church, our children will probably be equally critical and gossipy one day. And our spouse will resent the time we give to the church instead of feeling he or she is a partner in the joyful work of the gospel.

Speak as positively about the church as possible when you are at home. Talk about ministry as a joyful responsibility. Take your spouse and children along with you on hospital calls, home visits, and church activities. Be proud of God for what he is doing in the church local and universal. Because even in our darkest moments God is still at work. He is still pleased to use these broken "jars of clay" to bring new life to the world (2 Cor 4:7–12).

Chapter 16
Forgiveness

JOE HAD EVERY REASON for wanting to get back at them. Sure, he had made his share of mistakes. It was his unchecked egotism that had provoked them in the first place. He had deserved to be taken down a notch or two. Joe had been a dreamer, a goof-off, a spoiled brat. His boasting had antagonized them, not just once but several times. So when the opportunity presented itself they betrayed him—turned their backs on him, hung him out to dry. It was the worst form of cruelty. Thanks to them, he got in legal trouble and spent years languishing in prison. Not until his release did things finally begin to turn around.

Now, by the strangest set of circumstances, Joe's betrayers were standing right in front of him. No one would have blamed Joe if he had given them a taste of their own medicine. They were completely defenseless. He could have taken them to court or had them hauled off to prison or executed on the spot. But Joe didn't do any of that. Instead of justice, he gave them grace. Instead of getting even, he forgave them. He even opened his treasury and gave them the best of everything the land had to offer. Through the power of forgiveness, Joe and his former enemies were reconciled.

The story of Joseph in the Old Testament is inspiring, even spellbinding. It is also long; it occupies a full ten chapters of the book of Genesis. It's an honest drama about pride, jealousy, betrayal, injustice, reversal of fortune, love, honor, and grace. The climax of the story comes in Genesis 45 as Joseph reveals his identity to his eleven brothers. They had sold Joseph as a slave to Ishmaelite traders at least twenty years before. For all they knew, Joseph had died in some faraway land. Astonished that he is not only alive but the prime minister of Egypt, they fear he will order their execution. But Joseph forgives those who sold him into slavery and becomes a figure of the One who said from the cross, "Father, forgive them, for they know not what they do" (Luke 23:34).

In this section we are looking at the essential ingredients of recovery from the perils of pastoral ministry. We have seen that recovery requires faith in the gospel promises and reliance on the love of friends and family. Joseph's story confronts us with a final condition that is much more difficult. By God's grace we must forgive those who have hurt us. And, even harder, we must forgive ourselves.[1]

In the Bible, God commands us to forgive those who hurt us. One of Jesus' most familiar sayings is his reply to Peter in Matthew 18. Peter had asked Jesus, "Lord, how often will my brother sin against me, and I forgive him? As many as seven times?" Peter must have considered seven acts of forgiveness a lavish show of grace. But Jesus replied, "I do not say to you seven times, but seventy-seven times" (Matt 18:21–22). In other words, according to Jesus forgiving those who wrong us is always what Christians do. There is not a magic number of times beyond which it's okay for us to get revenge or write people off.

But what is forgiveness? Some people view forgiveness as the act of overlooking an offense or brushing it off. People will say to someone who hurt them, "Oh, don't worry about it; it's not a big deal." But ignoring, minimizing, or trying to forget about an

---

1. I am indebted to Dr. Timothy Keller, senior pastor of Redeemer Presbyterian Church in New York City, for the insights on gospel forgiveness contained in what follows.

offense is not forgiveness. Waiting until time has healed damaged emotions is not forgiveness. Yelling, throwing things, or pounding on a punching bag until we feel better is not forgiveness. Jesus defines forgiveness for us. After replying to Peter in Matthew 18, Jesus went on to tell a story about a merciful king who canceled a massive debt owed him by one of his servants. That servant then turned around and refused even to give one of his debtors time to work off his debt; instead, he threw him in prison. The point of the story, according to Jesus, is, "So also my heavenly Father will do to every one of you, if you do not forgive your brother from your heart" (Matt 18:23–35). Forgiveness, then, means doing what the merciful king did: canceling the debt incurred by a sinner and paying that debt ourselves.

Tim Keller explains,

> When someone seriously wrongs you, there is an absolutely unavoidable sense that the wrongdoer *owes* you. The wrong has incurred an obligation, a liability, a debt. Anyone who has been wronged feels a compulsion to make the other person pay down that debt. We do that by hurting them, yelling at them, making them feel bad in some way, or just waiting and watching and hoping that something bad happens to them. Only after we see them suffer in some commensurate way do we sense that the debt has been paid and the sense of obligation is gone. This sense of debt/liability and obligation is impossible to escape. Anyone who denies it exists has simply not been wronged or sinned against in any serious way. What then is forgiveness? Forgiveness means giving up the right to seek repayment from the one who harmed you. But it must be recognized that forgiveness is a *form of voluntary suffering*. What does that mean? Think about how monetary debts work. If a friend breaks my lamp, and if the lamp costs fifty dollars to replace, then the act of lamp-breaking incurs a debt of fifty dollars. If I let him pay for and replace the lamp, I get my lamp back and he's out fifty dollars. But if I *forgive him* for what he did, the debt does not somehow vanish into thin air. When I forgive him, I absorb the cost and payment for the lamp:

FORGIVENESS

either I will pay the fifty dollars to replace it or I will lose the lighting in that room. To forgive is to cancel a debt by paying it or absorbing it yourself. Someone always pays every debt.[2]

On the evening of June 17, 2015, a young man named Dylann Roof pulled out a .45-caliber handgun and shot nine people to death inside the historic Emanuel African Methodist Episcopal Church in Charleston, South Carolina. The nine were among a group of twelve adults and children participating in a midweek Bible study. Dylann Roof himself had been sitting in on the Bible study when he suddenly stood up and starting shooting while shouting racial epithets. Those killed ranged in age from twenty-six to eighty-seven.

The next morning, authorities apprehended Dylann Roof in Gastonia, North Carolina. On June 19 he appeared in Charleston County Court via videoconference for his bond hearing. At the hearing, survivors of the shooting and relatives of some of the victims spoke directly to Roof. One said, "You took something really precious from me. I will never talk to [my mother] again. I will never, ever hold her again. But I forgive you and have mercy on your soul. You hurt me. You hurt a lot of people. But God forgives you. I forgive you." The husband of one of the victims said, "I forgive you, and my family forgives you. But we would like you take [sic] this opportunity to repent. Change your ways." Another relative said, "I am a work in progress. I am very angry, [but] we are the family that love built. We have no room for hate, so I have to forgive."[3]

These words to the man who had brutally and casually ended the lives of their loved ones are an astonishing illustration of forgiveness. Notice that the survivors and relatives of the deceased acknowledged the immensity of the debt owed them. "You took

---

2. Keller, "Serving Each Other," 1–2.
3. Stableford, "Families of Charleston Shooting Victims to Dylann Roof: We Forgive You," lines 1–42.

something really precious from me," said one. "I am very angry," said another. To forgive does not mean to downplay the wrong that has been committed. In fact, just the opposite. True forgiveness can only occur when the seriousness of the sin and the cost of canceling the debt are recognized. An offer of cheap grace is not forgiveness. Think about Joseph. He did not say to his brothers, "Oh, it's no big deal that you sold me into slavery. I loved my years in prison." But neither did he demand payback. He paid the brothers' debt himself. He absorbed the cost of their sin. It is not just an extraneous detail that we're told that two times Joseph filled their sacks with grain, and both times put the money back in their sacks.

Those Charleston survivors and relatives set Dylann Roof free from their need for revenge. They paid the cost of Roof's sin. They relinquished him to the criminal justice system of South Carolina and to the mercy and justice of God, instead of destroying Roof with words or weapons of their own.

To absorb another's debt is a cost that must be counted. On the cross, Jesus knew both the seriousness of our sin and what it cost him to forgive us. Our sin was so serious it required nothing less than death—and that of the sinless son of God. What it cost Jesus was his descent into hell. Praise God that Jesus counted the cost and resolved to bear the wrath of God in our place.

Many of you picked up this book because you've been hurt in ministry. I'm going to guess that your story could have been told in these pages along with my story and those of Tony, Robert, James, Brent, Darren, Ben and Marlene, and Jonathan Edwards. You've been criticized, blamed, disrespected, lied to, or betrayed. You tried to lead; but people didn't want a leader, they wanted a compliant lap dog. You tried to be faithful to God and to your calling; but one storm after another has left you scarred, weary, and cynical. The people who said they'd be there for you, believed in you, and wanted you to be their pastor are nowhere to be found.

What do you do with these feelings? You can't ignore them, and time alone will not heal.

Forgiveness

You must do two things: Repent, and forgive.

Repent? Why must *we* repent if we've been hurt by others' sin? The reason is that "those people" are not the only sinners. "All have sinned and fall short of the glory of God" (Rom 3:23) is not just a verse to use in evangelism. You very likely have sinned against your church in some of the same ways your church has sinned against you. Jesus taught us to remove the plank from our own eye before we try to get the speck of sawdust out of someone else's eye (Matt 7:5). I had to repent of holding grudges against the elders of New Life Church and talking about them behind their backs. I had to repent of my poor leadership, weak faith, and inconsistent communication. I had to repent of making changes too quickly and ignoring the opinions and feelings of many church members. Even if your contribution to the problems at your church was five percent or less, you have sinned against your brothers and sisters in Christ. Admit your wrongdoing; don't shift blame or make excuses. If possible, go to the people you've offended, tell them what you did, and ask for their forgiveness. A refusal to own up to your part of the mess is not only going to short-circuit your recovery, it is a sign of pride. The gospel says, "You are more sinful than you could ever dare imagine and you are more loved and accepted than you could ever dare hope—at the same time."[4] God's adopting love for you frees you from the necessity of defending yourself because you've been fully justified already, not by your works but by Christ's.

Second, you must forgive.

To forgive does not necessarily mean to trust. When one person sins against another, until the sinner repents trust has been betrayed and must be rebuilt. Psychologist Dan Allender writes, "A forgiving heart cancels the debt but does not lend new money until repentance occurs. A forgiving heart opens the door to any who knock. But entry into the home, that is, the heart, does not

---

4. Tim Keller, Twitter post, June 13, 2013, 4:32 p.m., http://twitter.com/timkellernyc.

occur until the muddy shoes and dirty coat have been taken off."[5] Tim Keller adds,

> Forgiveness means a willingness to try to reestablish trust, but that reestablishment is always a process. The speed and degree of this restoration entail the re-creation of trust, and that takes time, depending on the nature and severity of the offenses involved. Until a person shows evidence of true change, we *should not* trust him or her. To immediately give one's trust to a person with sinful habits could actually be enabling him to sin. Trust must be restored, and the speed at which this occurs depends on the behavior.[6]

Also, to forgive does not guarantee that we suddenly feel better. Again, Keller offers this perspective:

> Forgiveness is not primarily a feeling, but a set of actions and disciplines. In summary, forgiveness is a promise *not* to exact the price of the sin from the person who wronged you. This promise means a repeated set of "payment" [sic] in which you relinquish revenge. It is hard and (for a while) constant. If this promise is kept actively, eventually the feeling of anger subsides. It is critical to realize at the outset, then, that forgiveness is not the forcing or denying of feelings, but a promise to make and to keep despite our feelings.[7]

Forgiving people means we will not keep bringing the matter up. We will be as kind as possible to the people who hurt us. We will pray for God to bless them. We will not go out of our way to avoid them. We will not criticize them before others. We will not think the worst thoughts about them, hope for their ruin, or celebrate their failures. We will stop playing recordings of hurtful incidents over and over in our mind. We will not indulge feelings of superiority over them. We will believe the gospel for them just as we believe the gospel for ourselves and our friends. We will hold

5. Allender, "Feeding Your Enemy," lines 126–128.
6. Keller, "Serving Each Other," 5.
7. Keller, "Love and Love Language," 12.

out hope for them. In all these ways, we will pay installments on their debt and willingly suffer instead of requiring them to suffer for their sin.

One of the persons we must forgive is ourselves.

Personally, I find it easier to let others off the hook than to let myself off the hook. I tend to remind myself of past failures. I think self-contemptuous thoughts. I am my own worst critic. I know what the gospel says, and I believe Jesus died for my sins. But like the man said at Dylann Roof's bond hearing, "I am a work in progress" when it comes to forgiving myself. I often resemble the father who said to Jesus, "I believe; help my unbelief!" (Mark 9:24). I find I must preach the gospel to myself throughout each day, lest I fall into a gaping Slough of Despond.

I draw great comfort from one word in the Greek New Testament: *tetelestai*. As most pastors know, that one word in Greek translates three words in most English Bibles: "It is finished" (John 19:30). On the cross, Jesus, "knowing that all was now finished" (John 19:28—again, the word *tetelestai*), paid our debt in full.

> Jesus paid it all,
> All to him I owe;
> Sin had left a crimson stain,
> He washed it white as snow.[8]

For believers in Jesus, not one sin will come back to haunt or judge us. Jesus was condemned so that we will not be. God promised, "For I will forgive their iniquity, and I will remember their sin no more" (Jer 31:34). He canceled our debt. Through faith in Jesus, we do not need to bring up the matter.

I carried an unforgiving spirit for several years after my resignation as the senior pastor of New Life Church. One Saturday afternoon I decided I'd lugged that weight of bitterness around long

---

8. Elvina M. Hall, 1865.

enough. I drove eighty miles to the church. Being a Saturday, no one was there. I parked in the back lot, turned off the engine, scanned the buildings and grounds, and revisited in my mind the five hard years I'd spent here as a pastor. I opened up the ledger of all my mistakes, admitted them to God, and asked his forgiveness. Then I opened up the other ledger. I acknowledged how I'd been hurt, blindsided, accused, and betrayed. Then I forgave New Life Church. How could I, who had been outrageously forgiven by God, do anything less? I relinquished the need for payback. I prayed for God to richly bless the pastors, the staff, the congregation, and the ministries of the church. I praised God for the lessons he had taught me there. I thanked him for the good times—there were many. I thanked him for the hard times too. And I raised my arms, opened up my hands, and let it all go.

As I sat in the church parking lot I recalled something Joseph had told his brothers. They were afraid that after their father Jacob died, Joseph would pay them back for selling him into slavery. They humbly asked for his forgiveness. Then Joseph reassured them with words about God's sovereignty: "'Do not fear, for am I in the place of God? As for you, you meant evil against me, but God meant it for good, to bring it about that many people should be kept alive, as they are today. So do not fear, I will provide for you and your little ones.' Thus he comforted them and spoke kindly to them" (Gen 50:19–21).

Even when storms of trouble and trial buffet the church, God is still in control. He knows what he's doing. What people intend for evil God intends for good. He's promised to build the church and not let the gates of hell prevail against it (Matt 16:18). Furthermore, he has promised to be with us through thick and thin, to the very end of the age.

> Fear not, I am with you, O be not dismayed;
> For I am your God, and will still give you aid;
> I'll strengthen you, help you, and cause you to stand,
> Upheld by my righteous, omnipotent hand.
> When through the deep waters I call you to go,

The rivers of sorrow shall not overflow;
For I will be with you, your troubles to bless,
And sanctify to you your deepest distress.
The soul that on Jesus has leaned for repose,
I will not, I will not desert to his foes;
That soul, though all hell should endeavor to shake,
I'll never, no never, no never forsake.[9]

By God's grace, it is possible to put the pieces back together and move forward in ministry after the storm has passed. Here is a recap of the Four Fs of recovery:

> **Summary of Part 3: Crisis Recovery**
>
> - Faith: Rest in God's unchanging love. Even in seasons of failure, you are God's beloved child.
> - Friends: Be intentional about finding and nurturing long-lasting friendships.
> - Family: Your family members will be there long after your church relationships end. Love and pastor them well.
> - Forgiveness: Release your church, and yourself, from the chains of bitterness and shame.

---

9. J. Rippon's *Selection of Hymns*, 1787.

Epilogue
Joy Comes in the Morning

More than a decade after Hurricane Katrina wreaked havoc and devastation upon the Gulf Coast, the Big Easy is still recovering. Signs are both encouraging and discouraging. Katrina changed the demographics of the city of New Orleans. According to the *New Orleans Advocate*, the city is "smaller and whiter even as its suburbs have become increasingly diverse." The report goes on to say that "newcomers have been flocking here in droves."[1] The number of Hispanic residents has increased dramatically. But the poverty rate is about the same as it was before the storm. And sadly, "[t]he quality of life for substantial numbers of black New Orleanians was a disaster before Katrina and appears to have worsened since then," say the authors of a 2014 essay in *The Times-Picayune*.[2] According to Erika McConduit-Diggs of the Urban League of Greater New Orleans, "When I look at what we've done throughout the city, I think most people would be amazed at the level of progress. But . . . when you dig a little deeper in terms of equity, in the recovery, that's where we're probably not as far as I'd like to see us be."[3]

People on the Gulf Coast begin many conversations with the phrases "before Katrina" and "after Katrina." For families like Phil

  1. Adelson, "Katrina Changes City's Ethnic Composition," lines 10–11, 95–96.
  2. *Times-Picayune*, August 29, 2014, lines 60–62.
  3. Adelson, "Katrina Changes City's Ethnic Composition," lines 85–88.

and Joy Steele and their two children, whom you met in the Introduction, life in Ocean Springs, Mississippi, is about the same as always. After Katrina, they returned to their home to find it nearly untouched. They were blessed. The same cannot be said for millions of other people.

Just as residents on the Gulf Coast can expect more hurricanes, I'll face more storms and disruptions in the churches that I serve. As I said in chapter 2, that's the way things are this side of heaven. But I'm wiser now. I have more tools to help me prepare for, endure, and recover from ministry storms than I've ever had. I've learned the truth of those words of the apostle James, "Count it all joy, my brothers, when you meet trials of various kinds, for you know that the testing of your faith produces steadfastness" (Jas 1:2–3).

After I resigned as pastor of New Life Church, I accepted a call to be the associate pastor in charge of adult ministries at another church in the same state. As I write, I have been here over fourteen years. My wife and I are empty nesters. Our marriage is strong, our kids are doing well, and I love vocational ministry. Soon I will have been an ordained minister for three decades. God has been gracious. Because of Jesus, I've done more than survive; I've thrived. I wouldn't trade pastoral ministry for anything.

I pray you will have the same experience.

Bibliography

Adelson, Jeff. "Katrina Changes City's Ethnic Composition." http://www.theneworleansadvocate.com/news/12479410-123/hurricane-katrina-transformed-new-orleans.
Allender, Dan B. "Feeding Your Enemy." https://bible.org/article/feeding-your-enemy.
———. *Leading with a Limp: Turning Your Struggles into Strengths.* Colorado Springs: Waterbrook, 2006.
Asghar, Rob. "Ranking the 9 Toughest Leadership Roles." http://www.forbes.com/sites/robasghar/2014/02/25/ranking-the-9-toughest-leadership-roles.
Bass, Peter, and Dean Borgman. "The Boston Miracle." http://www.urbanministry.org/wiki/boston-miracle.
Bentz, Rob. *The Unfinished Church: God's Broken and Redeemed Work-in-Progress.* Wheaton, IL: Crossway, 2014.
Bloom, Matt. "Well-Lived Pastoral Life: Summary of Results from the Initial Survey." PDF. South Bend, IN: Mendoza College of Business, University of Notre Dame, 2010.
Bounds, E. M. "Chapters 4–7." In *The Necessity of Prayer.* Cyber Library. http://www.leaderu.com/cyber/books/bounds/neco4-7.html.
Briggs, J. R. *Fail: Finding Hope and Grace in the Midst of Ministry Failure.* Downers Grove, IL: InterVarsity, 2014.
Brinkley, Douglas. *The Great Deluge: Hurricane Katrina, New Orleans, and the Mississippi Gulf Coast.* New York: HarperCollins, 2006. Kindle edition.
Brouwer, Mark. "The Friendless Pastor." http://www.christianitytoday.com/le/2014/march-online-only/friendless-pastor.html?start=1.
Brown, Jeffrey. "How We Cut Youth Violence in Boston by 79 Percent." Lecture, TED Talk, https://www.ted.com/talks/jeffrey_brown_how_we_cut_youth_violence_in_boston_by_79_percent?language=en.
Bunyan, John, and Barry E. Horner. *The Pilgrim's Progress.* Lindenhurt, NY: Reformation, 1999. http://bunyanministries.org/books/pp_full_text.pdf.

Bibliography

Bustanoby, Andre. "Wars You Can't Win." In *Leading Your Church through Conflict and Reconciliation: 30 Strategies to Transform Your Ministry*, edited by Marshall Shelley, 210–22. Minneapolis: Bethany House, 1997.

Calvin, John. *Institutes of the Christian Religion*. Translated by Robert White. Carlisle, PA: Banner of Truth Trust, 2014.

Collins, James C. *Good to Great: Why Some Companies Make the Leap—and Others Don't*. New York: HarperBusiness, 2001.

Crockett, Billy, and Kenny Wood. "The Day I Gave My Heart Away." Word Music, LLC, 1989.

Croft, Brian, and Cara Croft. *The Pastor's Family: Shepherding Your Family through the Challenges of Pastoral Ministry*. Grand Rapids: Zondervan, 2013.

DeYoung, Kevin. *Crazy Busy: A (Mercifully) Short Book about a (Really) Big Problem*. Wheaton, IL: Crossway, 2013. Kindle edition.

Doherty, Paul. "Science of Cycling: Aerodynamics & Drafting." https://www.exploratorium.edu/cycling/aerodynamics2.html.

Editorial. "The Battles of New Orleans." http://www.wsj.com/articles/the-battles-of-new-orleans-1440629569.

———. "Nine Years Post-Katrina, a Recovery Still in Progress: Editorial." http://www.nola.com/opinions/index.ssf/2014/08/nine_years_post-katrina_a_reco.html.

Edwards, Jonathan. "A Farewell Sermon." In *The Works of Jonathan Edwards*, edited by Edward Hickman, cc-ccvii. Vol. 1. Carlisle, PA: Banner of Truth Trust, 1974.

Gopnik, Alison. "In Life, Who Wins, the Fox or the Hedgehog?" http://www.wsj.com/articles/the-reality-behind-isaiah-berlins-fox-and-hedgehog-essay-1408144444.

Green, Lisa Cannon. "Research Finds Few Pastors Give up on Ministry." http://www.lifeway.com/pastors/2015/09/01/research-finds-few-pastors-give-up-on-ministry/.

Ivester, Lanier. "The Two Trees." http://www.thegospelcoalition.org/article/the-two-trees.

Keller, Timothy. *The Meaning of Marriage: Facing the Complexities of Commitment with the Wisdom of God*. New York: Riverhead, 2011.

———. "Serving Each Other through Forgiveness and Reconciliation." PDF. New York: Redeemer City to City, 2009.

———. "Session #1—Love and Love Language." Digital image. Redeemer.com. http://download.redeemer.com/pdf/Love_and_Love_Language.pdf.

Kennedy, Braga, et al. *Reducing Gun Violence: The Boston Gun Project's Operation Ceasefire*. US Department of Justice. Office of Justice Programs. https://www.ncjrs.gov/pdffiles1/nij/188741.pdf

Larson, Erik. *Isaac's Storm: A Man, a Time, and the Deadliest Hurricane in History*. New York: Random House, 1999.

Lewis, C. S. *A Grief Observed*. San Francisco: Harper Collins, 1994.

Bibliography

———. *The Voyage of the Dawn Treader*. In *The Chronicles of Narnia*, 419–541. New York: HarperEntertainment, 2005.

London, H. B., Jr., and Neil B. Wiseman. *Pastors at Greater Risk*. Ventura, CA: Gospel Light, 2003.

Luther, Martin. *A Commentary on St. Paul's Epistle to the Galatians*. Cambridge, Eng.: James Clarke, 1953.

Lynch, Robert P. "Building the Pillar of Trust." http://www.sigriddildine.com/The_Importance_of_Trust_V1.3.pdf.

Manning, Brennan. *Abba's Child: The Cry of the Heart for Intimate Belonging*. Colorado Springs: NavPress, 2002.

McIntosh, Gary, and Robert L. Edmondson. *It Only Hurts on Monday: Why Pastors Quit and What You Can Do about It*. Carol Stream, IL: ChurchSmart Resources, 1998.

Nagin, Ray C., and Kathleen Babineaux Blanco. Press Conference, MSNBC, et al, Aug. 28, 2005.

Nichols, Stephen J. *Jonathan Edwards: A Guided Tour of His Life and Thought*. Phillipsburg, NJ: P & R, 2001.

Nouwen, Henri J. M. *Here and Now: Living in the Spirit*. New York: Crossroad, 1994.

Piper, Barnabas. "Sinners in a Fishbowl." http://www.lifeway.com/pastors/2014/07/01/sinners-in-a-fishbowl.

Putnam, Robert D. *Bowling Alone: The Collapse and Revival of American Community*. New York: Simon & Schuster, 2000.

Rainer, Thom. "Nine Stupid Things I Did as a Pastor." http://thomrainer.com/2015/05/nine-stupid-things-i-did-as-a-pastor.

———. "Seven Ways the Pastor's Family Comes under Attack." http://thomrainer.com/2014/10/seven-ways-pastors-family-comes-attack.

Rainer, Thom S., and Eric Geiger. *Simple Church: Returning to God's Process for Making Disciples*. Nashville: Broadman, 2006.

Rowell, Edward. "Introduction." In *Leading Your Church through Conflict and Reconciliation: 30 Strategies to Transform Your Ministry*, edited by Marshall Shelley, 9–10. Minneapolis: Bethany House, 1997.

Sauls, Scott. "Sometimes, I Would Almost Rather Be Damned." http://scottsauls.com/2015/07/23/sometimes-i-would-almost-rather-be-damned.

Scazzero, Peter, and Warren Bird. *The Emotionally Healthy Church: A Strategy for Discipleship That Actually Changes Lives*. Grand Rapids, MI: Zondervan, 2003.

Shakespeare, William. *Hamlet*. Edited by George Steevens and Isaac Reed. In *The Dramatic Works of William Shakespeare in Eight Volumes*, edited by Samuel Johnson, 96–204. Vol. 8. New York: Harper and Brothers, 1905.

Shelley, Marshall. "Identifying a Dragon." In *Leading Your Church through Conflict and Reconciliation: 30 Strategies to Transform Your Ministry*, edited by Marshall Shelley, 60–71. Minneapolis: Bethany House, 1997.

———. *Well-Intentioned Dragons: Ministering to Problem People in the Church*. Waco, TX: Word, 1985.

Bibliography

Sherman, Daniel. "Pastor Burnout Statistics." http://www.pastorburnout.com/pastor-burnout-statistics.html.

Stableford, Dylan. "Families to Charleston Shooting Victims to Dylann Roof: We Forgive You." http://news.yahoo.com/familes-of-charleston-church-shooting-victims-to-dylann-roof--we--forgive-you-185833509.html.

Stetzer, Ed. "That Stat That Says Pastors Are All Miserable and Want to Quit (Part 1)." http://www.christianitytoday.com/edstetzer/2015/october/that-stat-that-says-pastors-are-all-miserable-and-want-to-q.html?utm_source=ctdirect-html&utm_medium=Newsletter&utm_term=9474670&utm_content=389124156&utm_campaign=2013.

Stetzer, Ed, and Warren Bird. "US Churches No Longer in Decline." http://catalystconference.com/read/us-churches-no-longer-in-decline.

Sweeney, Douglas A. *Jonathan Edwards and the Ministry of the Word: A Model of Faith and Thought.* Downers Grove, IL: IVP Academic, 2009.

Tavarez, Joon. "Wine Gets Better with Jesus, Not Age." http://www.driven.church/blog-minute-message-wine-gets-better-with-jesus-not-age.

Totman, Schuyler. *Ironies Leaders Navigate: What the Science of Power Reveals about the Art of Leadership and the Distinct Art of Church Leadership.* Eugene, OR: Wipf & Stock, 2014.

Tripp, Paul David. *Dangerous Calling: Confronting the Unique Challenges of Pastoral Ministry.* Wheaton, IL: Crossway, 2012.

Van Korlaar, Craig. "30+ Examples of Church Vision Statements." http://churchrelevance.com/30-church-vision-statements-examples.

Ver Merris, Dane, and Bert Van Hoek. "How Pastors Struggle." https://paulvanderklay.wordpress.com/2010/11/19/how-pastors-struggle.

Wagner, Philip. "The Secret Pain of Pastors." http://www.churchleaders.com/pastors/pastor-articles/167379-philip-wagner-secret-pain-of-pastors.html.

Walsh, Sheila, and Dave Cooke. "Jesus Loves the Church." Word Music, LLC, 1998.

Wikipedia contributors, "National Weather Service bulletin for Hurricane Katrina," Wikipedia, The Free Encyclopedia, https://en.wikipedia.org/w/index.php?title=National_Weather_Service_bulletin_for_Hurricane_Katrina&oldid=714988819 (accessed April 18, 2016).

Wikipedia contributors, "Operation Ceasefire," Wikipedia, The Free Encyclopedia, https://en.wikipedia.org/w/index.php?title=Operation_Ceasefire&oldid=708073829 (accessed April 18, 2016).

Wright, N. T. *Reflecting the Glory: Meditations for Living Christ's Life in the World.* Minneapolis: Augsburg, 1998.